Fantastic
Finishes

Fantastic *Finishes*

Paint effects and decorative finishes
for over 30 projects

NANCY SNELLEN

Chilton Book Company
Radnor, Pennsylvania

A QUARTO BOOK

Copyright © 1997 Quarto Inc.

ISBN 0-8019-8942-6

This book was designed and produced by
Quarto Publishing plc
The Old Brewery
6 Blundell Street
London N7 9BH

Senior art editor Antonio Toma
Designer Jane Forster
Editor Cathy Marriott
Text editors Maggi McCormick, Lynn Bresler
Managing editor Sally MacEachern
Photographers Ian Howes, Paul Forrester, Lyndon Parker
Picture researcher Natalie Rule
Picture manager Giulia Hetherington
Art director Moira Clinch
Editorial director Mark Dartford

Typeset in Great Britain by
Central Southern Typesetters, Eastbourne
Manufactured in Singapore by
Eray Scan Pte Ltd
Printed in Singapore by
Star Standard Industries Pte Ltd

Contents

Wood *Finishes*

Metal *Finishes*

Marble, Stone, and Shell *Finishes*

Decorative *Finishes*

Introduction

Whether you are touring ancient buildings in Europe or antebellum homes in the southern United States, among the embellishments gracing the castles and mansions of a bygone era are wonderful marble, granite, leather, and woodgrain furnishings. Upon close inspection you may discover that, while these items look and feel authentic, they are actually grand imitations.

The artists of yesteryear were masters in devising finishes that rivaled those of nature. Consequently, they were frequently commissioned to create magnificent faux-marble columns, floors, and statuary as well as beautifully grained furniture and other items for the wealthy owners. Faux, pronounced fo, is a French word which means unreal, not genuine: phony. The artists were so proficient in their field that today often the eye of the most experienced artisan is unable to determine the genuine from the counterfeit. Many of these imitations have been lovingly preserved and are still as beautiful as when they were produced.

Working with materials which were time-consuming and often hazardous to their health, it took years of practice for those great craftsmen to achieve the expertise

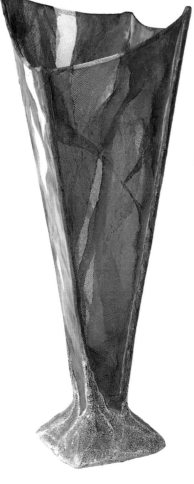

needed for quality workmanship. Today, however, even the beginning artist can create fantastic faux-finishes using the products made available by modern technology. Every dwelling can now be enhanced with beautiful faux-finish accents that cost little but look expensive.

Manufacturers are now providing artists with many new products designed especially for reproducing faux-finishes of the past. Health conscious and mindful of the environment, most of these products are non-toxic. Inexpensive kits which include everything necessary for professional looking results are available. Materials and tools are constantly being revised to simplify application so that even large projects can be finished in a few hours.

Those who love the look of aged wood no longer need to wait for days while the many coats of smelly glue and paint dry. No longer must a great deal of money be spent on beautiful woodgrain furniture. No longer must we only dream of owning elegant copper sculpture or marble statues. All this and more is now available to you with minimal expense, time, and effort.

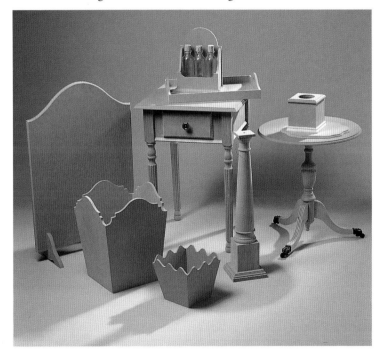

New stains in gel form, quick-drying wood sealers and varnishes, and new techniques are constantly being developed. Because of new mediums which retard drying time, acrylic paint can now be used for many projects which formerly required oil paints. Those who suffer from allergies to many of the older art materials usually find that they have no reaction to the new, user-friendly products.

Perhaps you prefer a modern decor rather than a country look, or possibly you love the elegance of Victorian furnishings. Whatever your preference, just follow the simple directions and let your imagination take you into a world of fantastic finishes.

Tools
and Materials

In this chapter we describe and outline the basic tools and materials used in this book. You probably already possess some of the equipment needed to create your own fantastic finishes. However, it is inevitable that you may require some specialist tools and materials to complete some projects. Fortunately, a wide range of products is available from local hardware stores or craft suppliers.

Filler Before sanding, sealing or painting a surface, you must fill any holes, gouges or other uneven areas with a filler to smooth the surface. There are a variety of fillers on the market and they are available in most craft or hardware stores. Follow the manufacturer's instructions to apply the filler. In most cases, you'll place some of the filler on the area to be filled then smooth it over with a palette knife. Scrape off the excess, then smooth over the area again and let dry.

Sandpaper Since the finished project will only be as good as the preparation, most wood projects require sanding with the grain for a fine surface. Unless the wood is very rough, a medium-to-fine sandpaper is usually sufficient.

Sealer Most wood projects should be sealed before paint is applied. The sealer helps the wood from drying out as well as helping to prevent excess moisture from penetrating the wood. To perform effectively, a sealer should be applied to a clean, dry surface and must be compatible with the paint to be applied over it. A water-based sealer is suitable for wood, plaster, papier-mâché, and other porous surfaces. It is a quick-drying sealer that dries to a clear, matte finish. When completely dry, the surface should be lightly sanded again for a smooth finish.

We recommend that you test products prior to using them on your project. Always work on a clean, flat surface and keep sharp implements beyond the reach of children. Spray varnishes are good for misting, or giving an even covering of varnish. Remember to spray in a well-ventilated room and to use sprays that are free from CFCs.

Take care when using materials containing solvents and other toxic substances – follow the manufacturer's instructions and take note of any safety recommendations. Always clean brushes and tools well immediately after use.

Tack Cloth This is a specially treated cloth used to remove dust and sanding residue from wooden painting surfaces. It is also a good idea to use a tack cloth to clean surfaces between coats of paint or varnish.

Glues Craft glue is a thick, white glue that dries fast and clear. It is used as a bonding agent on porous surfaces such as wood, paper, and ceramic. It can also be used as a sealer for paper or a decoupage finish. For gluing wood, specialist wood glues are fast drying. They bond tightly, cure in 24 hours, and can be sanded or painted.

Repositionable Adhesive Available in spray or an applicator bottle, this product provides a repositionable adhesive. Apply to the back of stencils or designs, and then place in position.

Masking Tape This is useful for protecting areas that should not be painted. Two or more rows can be used to create an open area of stripes in which paint may be applied. Edges of the tape should be pressed firmly down to bond to the surface and prevent paint from bleeding underneath.

Tracing Paper Tracing paper is a thin, transparent paper that allows the artist to see the underlying drawing. Lay a sheet of the tracing paper over a design and trace over the lines with a pen, pencil, or permanent marker.

Left
1 Disposable paper palette **2** Tracing paper
3 Stain **4** Wire brush **5** Graining tool
6 Disposable craft knife **7** Medium-fine
sandpaper **8** Sand **9** Synthetic sponge and
graining comb **10** A range of glues **11** Art
erasers **12** Masking tape **13** Furniture wax
14 Soft, lint-free cloth **15** Ruler
16 Repositionable adhesive

Transfer Paper Transfer paper is available in gray, white, red, yellow, and blue, but usually only gray or white is used. The transfer paper is laid on a surface with the dull side facing up. The traced design is then placed over the transfer paper and the pattern is transferred to the project by drawing over the design with a stylus.

Acrylic Paint This water-based, quick-drying paint provides good coverage on wood, papier-mâché, plaster, and bisque. The colors may be used as a base coat directly from the bottle or mixed together for custom colors. They may also be used for decorative painting. Clean up is easy with soap and water.

Transparent Spray Acrylic Paint Available in many colors as well as gold, silver, and copper, this spray is perfect for wood, fabric, foam products, baskets, silk flowers, and more. Clean up is easy with soap and water.

Gel Wood Stain This product can not only be used as a stain on raw wood, but can also be applied over painted surfaces as a semi-transparent glaze. While the gel is wet, a wood-graining tool can be used to create faux woodgrain. For staining, rub the gel into the wood with a soft, lint-free cloth.

Artist's Gel Thickener This is a water-based, clear thickener that can be used to create textures or a built-up look. It can be mixed with acrylic paints and applied to wood, bisque, tin, plaster, etc., with a brush or palette knife. It can be thinned with water, and tools can be cleaned with soap and water.

Acrylic Paint Retarder A medium that can be added to acrylic paint to slow down its drying time and to make it more transparent without losing its color.

Pickling Gel This transparent wash of color is especially nice on wood, as it allows the grain to show through. Apply the gel with a lint-free cloth and rub it into the wood.

Varnishes For most projects, quick-dry, non-toxic, water-based, brush-on varnishes of polyurethane acrylic are best, as they dry to a clear, durable finish. Matte varnish is best for those projects with a country or antique look. If you want a slight sheen, satin varnish is recommended. Gloss varnish produces a high sheen, and is recommended for granite and marble faux finishes, as well as other projects that require a high gloss.

Spray Varnish Spray varnishes are available in satin and gloss. Spray varnish provides fast-drying protection and should be applied lightly several times for best results.

Crackle Medium For the look of naturally aged wood, a light-to-heavy, even coat of crackle medium is applied over the base coat and allowed to dry until it becomes tacky. When a top coat of acrylic paint is brushed over the crackle medium, cracks will appear as the paint begins to dry. It is usually more attractive when a darker color is used for the base coat and a lighter one for the top coat. Apply the crackle horizontally for cracks going across the surface. Brushing up and down will create vertical cracks and a crisscross application will produce random cracking. *Note*: This crackle medium will *not* work on foil.

Left
1 A range of acrylic paints and gel wood stains
2 Acrylic spray paints **3** Water-based varnish, sealer, and acrylic paint retarder
4 Drawing pencils and white chalk pencil
5 Fabric paints **6** Stencil **7** Stencil paints
8 Stencil brush **9** Antiquing gel
10 Acrylic paints **11** Tube acrylic paints
12 Paper lace doily

13

TOOLS AND MATERIALS

Foil Crackle Medium Formulated especially for foil, this medium will not work with acrylic paints. It is applied over foil with a brush, and as the medium dries, random cracks form. Drying time will vary due to humidity and temperature.

Neutral Gel A medium to blend with acrylic paints to make them more transparent. It also slows down drying time.

Masking Fluid This product is drawn directly over the traced lines of a design on raw, painted, or pickled wood, and will prevent the area from being affected by stain or paint. When the painting is completed, the masking fluid is peeled away and the underlying surface is visible.

Stylus This is a pointed, metal tool used to transfer a pattern onto a surface. Once you've traced a pattern onto tracing paper, place a sheet of graphite paper between the tracing and the surface and gently run the tip of the stylus like a pencil over the traced pattern. The pressure on the stylus will cause the graphite to transfer to the surface, leaving an impression of the pattern.

Craft Foils Specialist craft foils are made especially for application on wood, papier-mâché, plastic, glass, and other hard surfaces. The look of gold, silver, or copper leaf is easy to achieve without the messy and time-consuming techniques formerly used. Foils are available in gold, silver, copper, red, green, and pearlized. Foils are also available in kit form.

Sponges Depending on the desired appearance, either synthetic or sea sponges work well with many faux finishes. A synthetic sponge has fine pores, while sea sponges have a larger, irregular pattern.

Stencil Paint Because this paint is solid, there is no dripping, and the risk of bleeding is lessened. Clean up with soap and water.

Graining Tools Available in an assortment of sizes and shapes, these tools are used for creating a realistic-looking woodgrain on any hard surface.

Brushes There are many different sizes and shapes of brushes, each of which has a special function. The content of the bristles is also important, and for acrylic painting a good synthetic brush is best. The following is a listing of brushes commonly used and their functions. A **sponge brush** is generally used for applying sealer, base coats, stains or finishes. A **flat brush** or **shader brush** is used for shading or highlighting. A **filbert brush** is shaped like a flat brush, but with a rounded tip, and is often used for decorative painting. A **fan brush** is shaped like a fan and is useful for painting foliage, grasses, feathers, etc. A **liner** is used for line work and tiny details. When made with long bristles, this brush is called a **script liner**. A **deerfoot brush** is a round, stubby brush with the tips of the brush cut at an angle. This brush is often used for painting fur, and grasses, etc. **Stencil brushes** are used for pouncing (stippling) color into the openings of a stencil. While there are many more brushes on the market, most painters find that they usually rely on several sizes of flat, round, and liner brushes. Most brushes can be used for a number of different techniques.

Right

1 Sponge brushes **2** A range of fan brushes, flat or shader brushes, base coating, and glazing brushes **3** Stencil brushes **4** A range of round, liner, flat or shader, filbert, deerfoot, angular, and dagger striper brushes **5** Crackle medium and acrylic paints **6** Foil kit (includes gold and mother of pearl/abalone foils, sealer, base coat, adhesive and antiquing gel) **7** Stencils

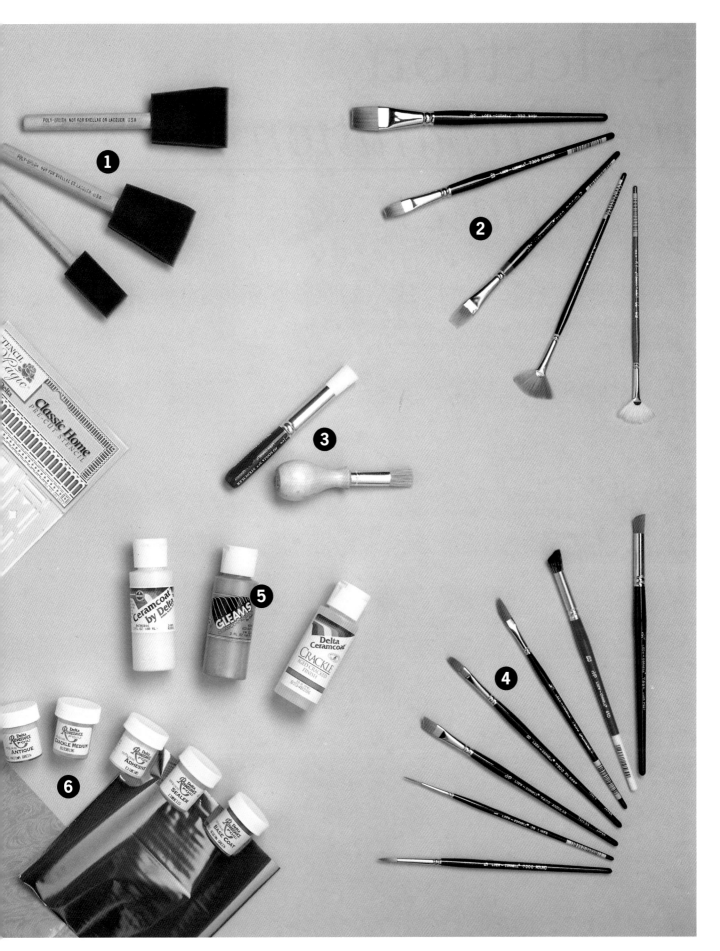

Selection and Preparation of Surfaces

It is often said that a finished project is only as good as the preparation. Not only does proper preparation determine the quality of the piece, but it makes a statement about the artisan. While preparation is often time-consuming work, the final effect is certainly worth the effort.

Before the actual preparation can begin, a surface must be selected. What will the purpose be – useful, decorative, or both? How much wear will the item be subjected to? Will it function as an interior or exterior object? Is it to be displayed in a traditional setting or a more contemporary area? These questions and more will need to be answered before the proper choices can be made.

While some surfaces will require more preparation than others, all surfaces lend themselves to fantastic finishes. For instance, if you choose an old metal piece, all rust must be removed and a protective finish applied to prevent further rusting before the actual decorating begins. On the other hand, papier-mâché can be decorated with a variety of finishes, and requires perhaps only a little sanding to remove rough spots.

When selecting wooden items, it is important to think about how they will be completed. If the wood is to be stained, it should be as free of blemishes as possible. A pretty grain is enhanced with stain, color washes, or pickling gels. Wood that will be painted can have more imperfections, and the grain pattern is not important as it will not show through the paint.

Right

Fantastic finishes can be applied to any shape or size of item. Here are a range of items that are suitable for paint finishing using the techniques described in this book.

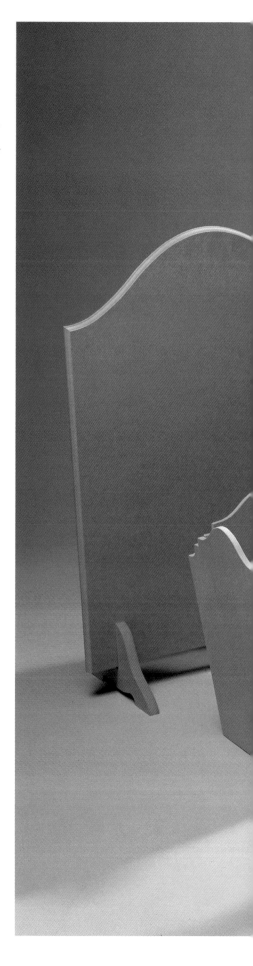

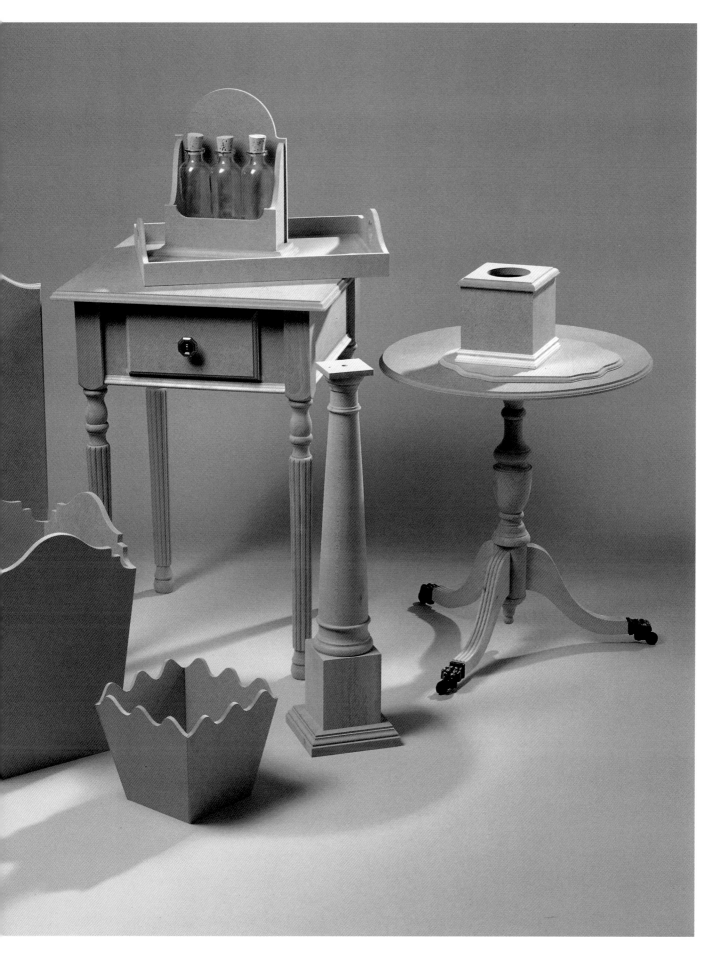

Regardless of the finish to be applied, any nail or staple holes or blemishes should be filled with a good wood filler that will accept stain or paint. All wood should be sanded with the grain, using a medium-fine sandpaper, and the residue wiped away with a tack cloth. A good quality sealer should then be applied, and after it has dried thoroughly, the wood should be lightly sanded with a fine sandpaper for a smooth finish.

Left

Before sanding, sealing, or painting a surface, you should fill any holes or uneven areas with a filler. Apply the filler with a palette knife.

Left

Before staining or painting, wood must be well sanded. Unless the wood is very coarse, a medium-fine sandpaper will remove the roughness and provide a good finish. Always sand with the grain of the wood.

If a piece is to be refinished, it is important to use materials compatible with the previous finish. If oil-based products were formerly applied to the raw wood, they may have penetrated the pores, and if this is the case, it may be impossible to remove all traces of the oil. Remember that oil and water do not mix, so an old, oil-based finish could prevent a solid bonding of the new finish being applied if it is a water-based acrylic. There are sealers made specifically for this situation, but if in doubt, it is best to choose oil-based products for the refinishing and decorating. On new wood there is no such problem, as it will readily accept water-based stains or paints.

If applying a stain to a wooden item, it is usually easier to control if the wood has been sealed. Sealer helps prevent the wood from drying out, shrinking, and cracking. It also helps to keep excess moisture from being absorbed into the wood, causing it to swell and bow.

Once the wood is properly prepared, a base of stain or paint can be applied. With the new water-soluble stain gels available, staining is no longer a messy process. The gels can be applied with a foam brush, old, lint-free rag, or even with a good quality, lint-free paper towel. The stain should be rubbed on in the direction of the grain, the excess wiped away, and allowed to dry thoroughly. When dry, should a darker color be desired, another application of stain can be made, repeating the above process. Clean up is easy with soap and water.

Most acrylic paints allow for a one-coat coverage. It is important to apply the paint evenly, using a damp brush, and often two thinner coats are better than one heavy one. If two coats are used, the first must be completely dry before the second is applied. Again, use soap and water for clean up.

For painting ease, it is good to seal all porous materials, such as plaster, with an appropriate sealer. This often will eliminate the necessity of applying several coats of the base color, as the sealer will inhibit excessive absorption of the paint.

Above

In order to prevent loss of moisture or additional moisture being absorbed, a good quality sealer must be applied to the raw wood and allowed to dry.

Once the base coat is dry, decorations such as stenciling, antiquing, foiling, and decorative painting can be done. When this process is completed and dry, a good quality finish should be used to protect the work. Matte, satin, or gloss varnishes are available, and the directions on the label should be read and carefully followed for best results. Again, if more than one application is used, drying time must be allowed between coats. The choice of sheen is a matter of individual preference, but consideration should be given to the piece, its use, and decoration before the selection of a varnish. For instance, a glossy finish does not enhance the look of weathered wood, so it is best to choose a matte varnish for such pieces. Foiled items often look best with a gloss finish, while satin finishes produce the look of a soft, hand-rubbed patina. An exterior varnish in satin or gloss should be used on pieces that will be subjected to weather.

The bottom, back, and inside of any surface should always be stained or painted, and finished in harmony with the rest of the piece. Often artists forget the importance of this step, but remember, until every section of a piece is completed, it is not finished!

With consideration for health and the environment, manufacturers are developing many more non-toxic products. They are constantly searching for good quality, easier-to-use materials, to make it possible for today's artist to create tomorrow's heirlooms.

Left

Clean all surfaces properly before painting to ensure that your paint finishes will withstand the effects of time.

Paint Finishes *Panel*

There are no limits to the wonderful effects that can be created with paints and a few simple tools. You can enliven virtually any surface or favorite object in your home. The final paint finish will depend on the surface material, the colors, and the paint technique used. For wood surfaces, it is often good to use just one color, as the grain of the wood will show through to create wonderful, unique patterns every time. Alternatively, try combining two or more paint colors. The final color is the result of an optical combination rather than the direct physical mixture of the paint, and the effect is often quite luminous. Or, you can try using paint to

WOOD FINISHES

Light blue wood stain

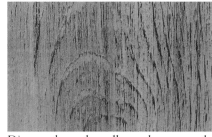
Distressed wood – yellow ocher over red

Natural brown wood stain

METAL FINISHES

Metallic finish – red oxide and gold

Textured metal finish

Verdigris – dragging paint effect

MARBLE, STONE, AND SHELL FINISHES

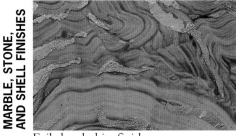
Foiled malachite finish

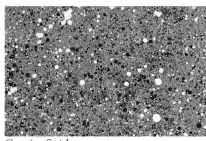
Granite finish

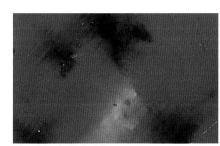
Tortoiseshell finish

DECORATIVE FINISHES

Decoupaged and painted tissue paper

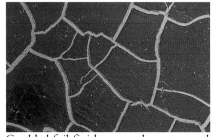
Crackled foil finish – complementary red and gold

Textured paint finish – using sand

copy beautiful, natural patterns such as marble, granite, verdigris, malachite, etc. When copying natural finishes, it is a good idea to have a photograph to hand for reference, as this will make your painting easier and more accurate. Here are a range of ideas for a variety of wood, metal, marble, stone, shell, and decorative finishes.

Don't be afraid to experiment and adapt techniques. Part of the fun with decorative finishes is that each time you experiment, you will create an original style and look. Most techniques can be adapted for a variety of materials and objects, and each project should be regarded as starting point to stimulate your imagination.

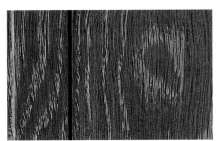
Pickled wood finish

Distressed wood – navy blue over red

Viridian green wood stain

Crackled foil finish – black and silver

Verdigris – sponging and spattering paint effect

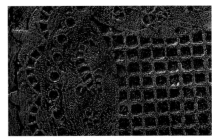
Textured gilt finish – using a paper lace doily

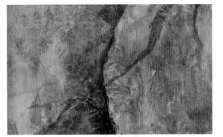
Fantasy green marble finish

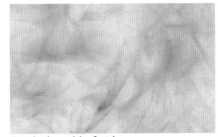
Smoked marble finish

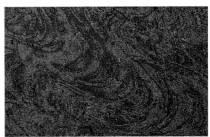
Pearlized finish

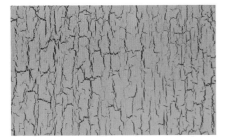
Crackle glaze – yellow ocher over red

Crackle glaze over decoupage

Leather-look finish

21

PAINT FINISHES PANEL

PREPARATION
OF WOOD IS VERY
IMPORTANT. IT IS VITAL THAT
THE WOOD BE PROPERLY DRIED AS
GREEN WOOD USUALLY WARPS AND/OR
CRACKS. IT IS ALSO IMPORTANT THAT WOOD BE
SEALED WITH A GOOD QUALITY SEALER TO PREVENT THE
LOSS OF NATURAL MOISTURE AND THE ABSORPTION OF
ADDITIONAL MOISTURE. WITH TODAY'S PRODUCTS, IT IS POSSIBLE TO

Wood Finishes

CREATE SPECIALTY EFFECTS ON WOOD WHICH HAS LESS THAN DESIRABLE GRAIN OR COLOR.
WHILE THERE IS AN INHERENT BEAUTY TO NATURAL WOOD WITH A HAND-RUBBED
PATINA, THERE IS ALSO CHARM IN WORN, AGED WOOD AND WEATHERED WOOD
WITH ITS CRACKED, PEELING PAINT. COLORED STAINS, AS WELL AS PAINT,
CAN ADD INTEREST TO AN OTHERWISE NONDESCRIPT ITEM. IN THIS
CHAPTER WE WILL INTRODUCE YOU TO AN ASSORTMENT OF
FINISHES, REALISTIC AS WELL AS FANTASY. YOUR
IMAGINATION IS THE ONLY LIMIT AS YOU
BEGIN YOUR ARTISTIC EXCURSION INTO
A WORLD OF WOOD.

Decoupaged *Fireplace Screen*

THIS BEAUTIFUL FIREPLACE SCREEN WOULD BE PERFECT IN THE MOST ELEGANT ROOM. CHOOSE YOUR FAVORITE SONG AND DECOUPAGE THE SHEET MUSIC TO WOOD PIECES.

YOU WILL NEED
Fireplace screen
Sandpaper
Sealer
Tack cloth
Deep brilliant red and ivory acrylic paint
1in (2.5cm) glaze/wash brush
Ruler
½in (1cm) masking tape
White chalk pencil
Craft glue
Wrapped column stencil
Repositionable adhesive spray
Brayer or rolling pin (optional)
Disposable acrylic paper palette
Brown antiquing gel
Gold stencil oil-based paint
1in (2.5cm) stencil brush
Satin spray varnish
Soft cloth or lint-free paper towels

1 Sand and seal the entire screen. When dry, sand lightly to remove the raised grain and wipe with a tack cloth to remove the residue. Apply the deep brilliant red base coat and let it dry thoroughly. If a second coat is needed for good coverage, it can be applied when the first coat is dry.

2 With the chalk pencil and the ruler, mark lines 2in (5cm) from the edge around the fireplace screen. Draw the lines as lightly as possible.

3 Place masking tape along the outside of the drawn lines. Press firmly with the fingertips to seal the edges of the tape to prevent the glue from bleeding into the border area. Cut the sheet music to fit inside the masked area. After cutting each piece, check to see that it fits close to the masking tape lines without going over them.

4 Working quickly, brush glue within the masked area. For easier application thin the glue with a little water. Position the sheet music. Press and rub firmly but carefully to remove any air pockets or wrinkles. You may want to use a brayer or rolling pin for this. Let the glue dry completely before sealing the music with one or two coats of glue. Be sure to cover the edges of the music and allow drying time between applications.

5 Remove the tape from the board carefully. Lightly spray the sheet music with satin varnish and let it dry. Spray the back of the stencil with repositionable adhesive. When it is tacky but not wet, blot with a paper towel. Position the stencil in place on the border.

6 Fill the bristles of the stencil brush with ivory. Blot the excess on a towel, then pounce (stipple) on the color. Reposition the stencil and repeat the entire process until all the panels are finished.

7 Place masking tape along the edges of the sheet music. Press another row of tape along the edge of the border, leaving ¼in (5mm) space between the two rows of tape. In this space apply the gold stencil paint with the soft cloth or lint-free paper towel.

8 Carefully remove the tape so as not to damage the sheet music. Spray the music and the board lightly with satin varnish.

9 When the varnish is dry, antique over the entire screen with the brown antiquing gel applied with a brush, soft cloth or paper towel. Wipe away the excess, completing one panel at a time until all are done. Allow to dry and then finish the screen with satin varnish.

Mini Chest of Drawers

JUST THINK OF ALL THE TRINKETS YOU

COULD STASH IN THIS WONDERFUL LITTLE WOODEN CHEST!

THE DESIGN IS SIMPLE AND WOULD LOOK LOVELY IN ANY ROOM.

1 Sand and seal all areas of the chest. When dry, lightly sand again and wipe away the residue with the tack cloth. Base coat the entire chest with ivory paint, covering well. When dry, spray a light coat of varnish over all painted areas.

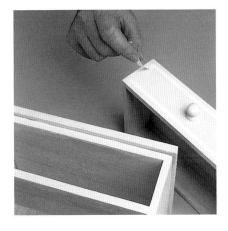

2 Measure and lightly mark a ¼in (5mm) border around the drawers and top of the chest. Cut strips of masking tape and press the tape firmly along the lines. Be sure the tape is securely bonded to the wood to prevent bleeding.

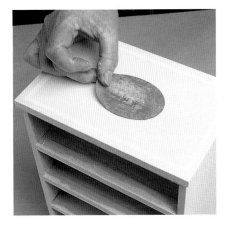

3 Cut an oval shape from the sheet of plastic. Spray one side with repositionable spray adhesive and when the glue is sticky but not wet, pat with a soft cloth to remove any excess. Position the oval in the center top of the chest, and with the fingers, press firmly around the edges for a good seal.

YOU WILL NEED
Small wooden chest of drawers
Wood sealer
Sandpaper
Tack cloth
Base-coating brush, small round brush, 1in (2.5cm) stencil brush
Ivory, olive green, cadmium red medium, and gray-green acrylic paints
¼in (5mm) masking tape
Mixing knife
Disposable acrylic paper palette
1 sheet of stiff, semi flexible, medium weight plastic
Repositionable spray adhesive
Neutral gel
Satin spray varnish
Ruler
Black permanent marking pen
Tracing paper
Transfer paper
Stylus
Furniture wax
Olive green oil-based stencil paint
Lint-free cloth

TIP . . .
Before marking the areas with a pen, cut around the stripes and the circle with a craft knife. This will help prevent bleed out and enhance the aged appearance.

4 Mix some neutral gel into olive green paint for a transparent color. Use the stencil brush and pounce (stipple) the color over the painted chest and let it dry.

6 Sand to remove some of the paint for an antique look. More paint can be sanded away if you desire an older look. For a less aged appearance, less sanding is required.

5 Remove both the tape and the oval template from the chest.

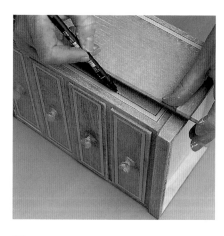

7 Using the ruler as a guide, draw lines around the bands and the oval with the permanent marking pen. Trace the scallops and triangles onto tracing paper and transfer them to the chest using the transfer paper and the stylus.

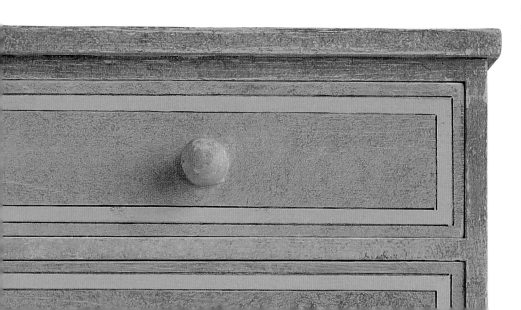

WOOD FINISHES

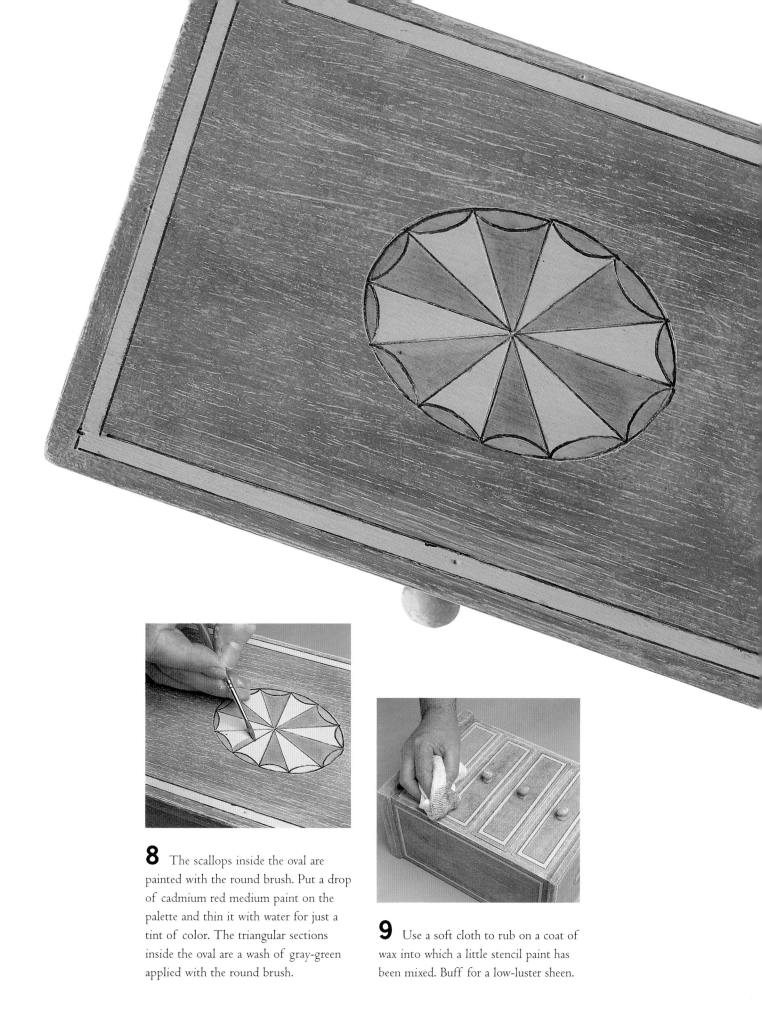

8 The scallops inside the oval are painted with the round brush. Put a drop of cadmium red medium paint on the palette and thin it with water for just a tint of color. The triangular sections inside the oval are a wash of gray-green applied with the round brush.

9 Use a soft cloth to rub on a coat of wax into which a little stencil paint has been mixed. Buff for a low-luster sheen.

Magazine Holder

BLACK AND WHITE PHOTOCOPIES OF A FAVORITE PHOTO OR PICTURES FROM MAGAZINES ARE USED TO CREATE THIS HEIRLOOM THAT WILL BE TREASURED FOR YEARS TO COME.

YOU WILL NEED
Wooden magazine holder
Sandpaper
Wood sealer
Soft lint-free cloth
Black and cream acrylic paint
1in (2.5cm) glazing brush,
½in (1cm) flat brush
Photocopied magazine cutouts
Craft glue
Cold coffee or tea
Coffee granules
Crackle medium
Sealer
Brush-on antique-colored tinted varnish
Scissors

1   Sand and seal all surfaces. When dry, lightly sand again and wipe away the residue. With the 1in (2.5cm) brush, base coat all but the insert with black. (*Do not* paint inside the side grooves in order to allow the insert to slide in and out easily.) Set aside and let it dry. Paint the front panel using the cream paint. Again, let it dry.

2   Using scissors, carefully cut out the photocopies of your pictures, here we have used silhouettes, a house and oval frames. Position the cutouts on the front panel, and glue in place using craft glue. Allow the glue to dry, then brush an even coat of glue horizontally over the pictures. When this is dry, brush on another even coat of glue in a vertical direction. Allow this to dry completely before proceeding to the next step.

3   "Age" the front panel all over with cold coffee or tea using a soft cloth. Speckle a few coffee granules randomly around to create age specks or fly spots.

4   Brush crackle medium over the black paint, following the directions on the package. Paint over the crackle medium with cream paint. As the paint dries, cracks will form almost immediately. Let it dry. Drying time will vary due to humidity and temperature. Spray sealer over the crackled area, and let it dry.

5   Carefully remove any excess coffee granules from the front panel using a soft cloth. Then brush tinted varnish over the entire holder, including the front panel, to "age" it.

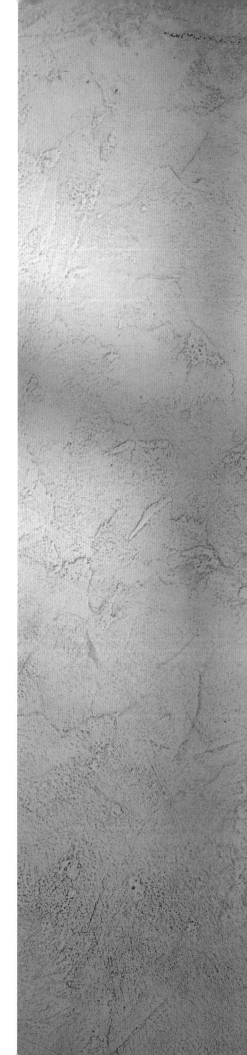

Hanging *Kitchen* *Rack*

THIS NEAT LITTLE SHELF WOULD MAKE A WELCOME ADDITION TO ANY KITCHEN. IT IS EASY TO MAKE, BUT THE DECORATING DIRECTIONS COULD BE ADAPTED TO A PURCHASED SHELF AS WELL.

YOU WILL NEED
Wooden shelf
Fine sandpaper
Tack cloth
Dark green, burgundy, and cream acrylic paint
2in (5cm) and 1in (2.5cm) flat paint brush, ½in (1cm) liner brush
Antique-colored furniture paste wax
Steel wool
Ruler
Brush-on varnish
Antiquing gel
Soft, lint-free cloth
Wooden knobs or pegs

2 Using the smaller, 1in (2.5cm) brush, carefully brush on the paste wax in random, occasional streaks, where you would expect to see wear and tear. Allow the unit to dry overnight.

1 Sand the shelf with fine sandpaper and wipe away the residue with the tack cloth. Base coat the entire unit using dark green paint and the 2in (5cm) brush. Let the paint dry.

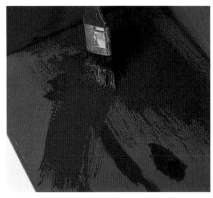

3 With the 2in (5cm) flat brush, paint the entire shelf with bur- gundy paint. Let it dry thoroughly before proceeding to the next step.

4 With the steel wool, create a dis- tressed appearance by rubbing over the entire surface, using more pressure here and there for an antique effect.

5 Using the ruler as a guide for the crisscross pattern, freehand the design on both sides of the shelf and along the top with the ½in (1cm) liner brush and cream paint. Lightly sand over the pat- tern when the paint is thoroughly dry. Wipe away the sanding dust with the tack cloth.

6 With the soft, lint-free cloth, rub antiquing gel over the crisscross design to age the cream paint. Wipe away any excess. When the gel is dry, repeat this process if more antiquing is desired.

7 Brush the varnish carefully over the patterning. Let it dry thoroughly.

9 Finally, screw in the knobs along the bottom edge of the shelf unit.

8 Using the dark green paint, carefully paint the knobs or pegs. Allow them to dry completely.

Antiqued
Chessboard

IF YOU LIKE TO PLAY CHESS, YOU WILL LOVE THIS
GAME BOARD. IT IS EASY TO MAKE — YOU JUST NEED A
24IN (60CM) SQUARE BOARD WITH BEVELED EDGES AND
A FEW SUPPLIES. IN NO TIME AT ALL, YOU WILL
COMPLETE THIS USEFUL AND DECORATIVE ITEM.

YOU WILL NEED
Chessboard
Sandpaper
Wood sealer
Tack cloth
Ruler
White chalk pencil
Masking tape
Ivory and gray-green acrylic paint
1in (2.5cm) stencil brush, large flat
brush, 1in (2.5cm) glazing brush,
2in (5cm) flat paint brush
Gold oil-based stencil paint
Repositionable adhesive spray
Brown antiquing gel
Arch stencil
Soft lint-free cloth
Paper towels
Satin spray or brush-on varnish

WOOD FINISHES

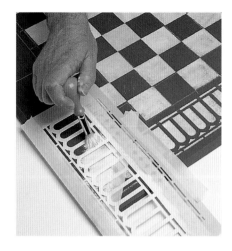

1 Sand and seal the entire chessboard. When it is dry, lightly sand to remove any raised grain and wipe with a tack cloth to remove the sanding dust. Base coat the entire board with gray-green, using the 2in (5cm) flat brush.

3 Load the stencil brush with ivory, blot the excess on a paper towel, and stipple (pounce) color into every other square, being careful not to get paint into the next square. (This is easier if a stencil is used.) A little of the background should show through the stippled squares.

4 Spray the back of the arch stencil with repositionable spray adhesive. Let it dry until it feels tacky, then blot with the cloth. With the stencil brush and ivory paint, stipple color over the arches as you did in the squares. Carefully remove the stencil and reposition it, repeating the instructions above until you have completed the border around the board.

WOOD FINISHES

2 Using a ruler and a chalk pencil, measure and mark a 4in (10cm) border around the board; 2in (5cm) squares are then measured and marked on the surface of the board.

5 Place a row of masking tape along the outer edge of the squares. Keeping the tape straight, place another row of tape ½in (1cm) from the edge of the first row. Press firmly with the fingers to seal the edges of the tape and prevent paint from bleeding under the edges.

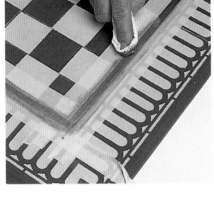

6 With the cloth, rub the gold stencil paint into the open area between the two pieces of tape. Continue until you have completed the entire board. Use as much or as little gold as you like.

7 Carefully lift off the tape and allow the stencil paint to dry. Highlight the stenciled design by laying the stencil over the border and rubbing stencil paint over the arches. The squares may also be done in this manner. This is a highlight – so don't overdo it. Trim the board by rubbing stencil paint along the edge.

8 Brush or spray the surface of the board with a light coat of satin varnish. When it is dry, use the large flat brush and antique the board with brown antiquing gel. Rub away any excess with a soft cloth and allow it to dry thoroughly. Re-apply the antiquing gel if desired.

9 Brush or spray the entire board with a light coat of satin varnish. When dry, apply another light coat of varnish and dry completely. Repeat until you have achieved the desired finish.

WOOD FINISHES

TIP
Never use oil brushes in acrylic paints as this will ruin them for painting in oils in the future.

Distressed
Wood
Coat *Rack*

YOU WILL HAVE NO PROBLEM GETTING

THE CHILDREN TO HANG UP THEIR

COATS WHEN THEY SEE THESE

CHEERFUL LITTLE BIRDIES JUST

WAITING FOR THEM. AFTER YOU

PAINT THIS AS SHOWN, PAINT ONE

FOR EACH CHILD'S ROOM IN COLORS

TO MATCH THE DECOR.

43

YOU WILL NEED
Wooden coat rack
Wire brush
Soft lint-free cloth
Tracing paper
White transfer paper
Pen or pencil
Stylus
Eraser
1in (2.5cm) glazing brush, large
shader, medium round brush, small
script liner
Oxide red and cadmium yellow deep
acrylic paints
Navy blue pickling gel
Black ballpoint pen
Wood glue
Spray or brush-on varnish

2 With pressure, create texture on the board by rubbing the bristles of the wire brush back and forth along the length of the board.

1 Remove the pegs from the coat rack and set aside. Using red oxide and the 1in (2.5cm) brush, base coat the board. Let the paint dry.

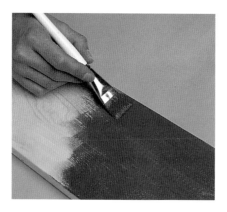

3 Wipe the board to remove any residue, then brush the navy blue pickling gel over the surface.

4 Use a soft cloth and pressure to rub the gel into the grooves. Wipe away the excess and let the gel dry before proceeding to the next step.

5 Again, use the wire brush, but with less pressure than in step 2, to rub randomly and briskly along the length of the board to create more grooves.

6 With the shader, streak navy blue pickling gel over the board and let it dry.

8 Use the round brush to paint the birds with cadmium yellow deep. For good coverage apply another coat of paint after the first one has dried. Thin

red oxide with water so it will flow from the brush easily. Fill the bristles of the script liner brush with the paint and, holding the brush vertically, outline the birds carefully.

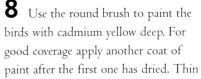

7 Trace the bird design on tracing paper and transfer it to the board using the transfer paper and stylus. Go over the traced lines with the black ballpoint pen. Erase any white lines left from transferring the design.

9 Paint the pegs with red oxide. When dry, apply glue to one end of each peg and insert the pegs into the holes of the board. When the paint and glue have dried completely, finish with spray or brush-on varnish.

Faux Woodgrain Umbrella Holder

PURCHASE AN UNFINISHED, READYMADE UMBRELLA HOLDER — AND DECORATE IN THE COLORS HERE OR CHOOSE OTHERS TO HARMONIZE WITH YOUR HOME DECOR.

1 Base coat the umbrella holder with white paint. Apply a second coat of paint if needed after the first is dry. Then, pour 1 part of medium red paint and 15 parts of neutral gel into a glass jar. Stir with the wooden end of a brush, mixing well.

2 Lay the umbrella holder on a table and, working on one side at a time, brush on the gel and paint mixture. The color will be transparent, but be sure the entire area is well covered.

3 While the paint is wet, move the wood-graining tool downward, slightly rocking it back and forth to create a woodgrain appearance. If you do not like the design, brush on more of the paint mixture and use the graining tool again. Complete a second side and let it dry, then repeat these instructions for the other two sides. Again, let the paint dry.

YOU WILL NEED
Umbrella holder
Neutral gel
White, medium red and black acrylic paint
Glass jar
1in (2.5cm) glazing brush, and ½in (1cm) flat brush
Wood-graining tool
Spray or brush-on satin or gloss varnish

4 With the ½in (1cm) brush and black paint, trim the top and bottom bands. If necessary for total coverage, apply a second coat when the first coat is completely dry. Let that dry, then finish with brush-on or spray varnish. Use several coats of varnish on the inside to prevent damage from dripping umbrellas.

Topiary Tree

L ET YOUR HORTICULTURAL IMAGINATION RUN WILD AND CREATE THIS FANTASY TREE TO GRACE YOUR SUNROOM OR PATIO. MAKE IT YOURSELF OR, IF YOU ARE NOT ADEPT WITH TOOLS, HAVE A WOOD CUTTER DO IT FOR YOU.

YOU WILL NEED
¼in (5mm) plywood or pressed wood, cut to shape – see step 1
Saw
Tape measure
Sandpaper
Tack cloth and soft, lint-free cloth
Dark green, pale cream, yellow ocher, white, lemon yellow, emerald green, terracotta, and olive green acrylic paint
Disposable acrylic paper palette
Mixing knife
2in (5cm) and 1in (2.5cm) flat brush, ½in (1cm) stencil brush
Foam- or rubber-backed carpet
Craft knife
Strong waterproof glue
Crackle medium
Geometric stencil
½in (1cm) masking tape
Neutral gel
Wood-graining tool or brush
Crackle varnish
Light brown gel stain
Oil-based matte varnish
Wood screws
Ribbon

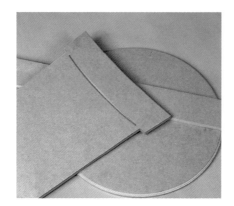

1 Cut out a 15in (38cm) circle, a 10in (25cm) by 12in (30cm) pot shape, and a stem shape 3in (7.5cm) by 36in (91cm) from the plywood or pressed wood. Sand all the pieces and wipe away the residue with the tack cloth. Base coat the circle with dark green, the stem with pale cream, and the pot with yellow ocher, using the 2in (5cm) brush. Allow to dry thoroughly.

TIP
When mixing dark and light colors of paint it is best to mix the darker shade into the lighter shade. This eliminates mixing more paint than is needed in order to arrive at the correct color.

2 Cut five leaf shapes and a lemon shape out of the foam- or rubber-backed carpet, using a craft knife. Glue the shapes carpet-side down onto scraps of wood. The wood helps create even pressure when printing the shapes onto the dark green fiberboard circle.

3 You will need three shades of green. Pour three puddles of white onto the palette, add a different amount of dark green to each, mixing well with the mixing knife. With the 1in (2.5cm) brush, paint the foam leaf shapes in the three shades of green, emerald green, and white. Paint the lemon foam shape in lemon yellow.

4 Print the leaf and lemon shapes randomly onto the dark green fiberboard circle, reloading the foam pads with paint as necessary. Overlap the lighter colors over the darker colors in places. Leave the circle to dry.

5 With the 2in (5cm) brush, apply the crackle medium to the pot, following directions on the label for application and drying time. Brush terracotta over the medium, applying quickly and in one direction. As the paint begins to dry cracks will form, so do not go into the painted areas again. Allow to dry.

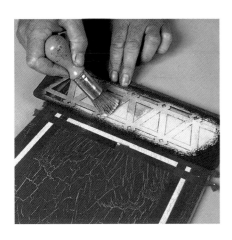

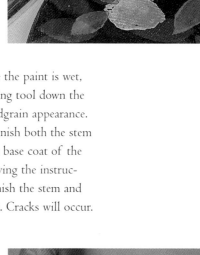

6 Place the stencil at the lower edge of the pot, and apply cream paint with the stencil brush. Place masking tape along the top edge of the stencil, and also 1in (2.5cm) in from the edge on the other three edges. Place a second row of masking tape ½in (1cm) inside the first row. Press down the tape firmly.

8 Mix neutral gel with olive green paint, and paint the stem using the 1in (2.5cm) brush. While the paint is wet, move the wood-graining tool down the stem, to create a woodgrain appearance. Leave to dry, then varnish both the stem and the tree using the base coat of the crackle varnish, following the instructions. When dry, varnish the stem and tree with the top coat. Cracks will occur. Leave to dry.

7 Using the stencil brush and the cream paint, stencil color between the two rows of tape. Once dry, remove the tape carefully.

9 With a soft, lint-free cloth, rub light brown gel stain over the stem and tree. With a clean area of the cloth, wipe away any excess and allow to dry. Varnish all pieces, then complete the tree by screwing the three pieces together and adding a decorative ribbon.

Wood Finishes Gallery

Wooden Box (above)

Cherry and walnut gel stains were rubbed into the sanded, raw wood box. Masking tape was used to create a pattern for areas to be stained or painted, and to cover areas that were not stained.

Wood-stained Chest of drawers (left)

Staining with bold, vivid colors can make wood dramatic. The use of water-based glazes makes staining easy and attractive. Try staining in colors other than wood tones; the look is often unusual.

Decorative Shelf (right)

Forest green pickling gel was applied to the sanded, raw wood frame. The insert was stenciled, then cutouts of the pattern were laid over the stenciled areas. Then pickling gel, thinned with water, was spattered over the surface.

Crackled Chair (left)

One thing that time does is cause a surface or varnish to crack. These cracks usually add a certain charm to a piece, making it much more visually interesting. Fortunately, we no longer have to wait for time to provide crackle finishes; here, the artist has created an aged appearance using a crackle medium.

Pickled Oak Box (below)

Many hardwoods used to be treated with lime to protect them from destructive pests that ravaged buildings and furniture. However, the familiar white grain of treated wood has now become popular, and can be achieved easily with pickling wax. A layer of pickling wax was applied to this box with steel wool. When dry, a little clear furniture wax was added, and then buffed to a mid sheen finish with a soft cloth.

53

Metal Finishes

THE ART OF
METAL WORK IS A TIME
CONSUMING, EXPENSIVE
UNDERTAKING — BUT USING A
VARIETY OF PAINTING TECHNIQUES, IT IS
POSSIBLE TO CREATE A RANGE OF WONDERFUL
METAL FINISHES. TODAY IT IS POSSIBLE TO TRANSFORM
THE COMMON INTO THE UNCOMMON. QUICK AND EASY-TO-USE,
SUCH PRODUCTS ARE OFTEN MARKETED IN KIT FORM, AND BY FOLLOWING

THE SIMPLE DIRECTIONS ON THE PACKAGE, YOU CAN CREATE A "MASTERPIECE" IN A FEW HOURS.
REALISTIC FOILS ARE AVAILABLE IN GOLD, SILVER, AND COPPER AND DIRECTIONS FOR USE
ARE UNCOMPLICATED. THEY ARE ALSO INEXPENSIVE, AND CAN BE APPLIED TO ANY
HARD SURFACE. PAINTS AND ANTIQUING MEDIUMS CAN GIVE NEW LIFE TO
FORMER "THROWAWAYS." IN THIS CHAPTER WE HAVE PROVIDED
YOU WITH A VARIETY OF FINISHES USED ON A NUMBER OF
DIFFERENT SURFACES. THIS IS ONLY THE BEGINNING,
HOWEVER, AS YOU ARE SURE TO THINK OF
MANY MORE WAYS TO CREATE
METALLIC FINISHES.

IF YOU LOVE FUN PROJECTS, THIS ONE IS FOR YOU. PURCHASE A WOODEN FRAME, A FEW BASIC SUPPLIES, AND IN NO TIME YOU CAN COMPLETE THIS DELIGHTFUL FRAME SUITABLE FOR A MIRROR OR YOUR FAVORITE PHOTO.

Verdigris *Mirror Frame*

YOU WILL NEED
Mirror or picture frame
White, Payne's gray, and phthalo green acrylic paints
Copper metallic acrylic paint
1in (2.5cm) glazing brush, medium round brush, 1in (2.5cm) stencil brush
Sea sponge
Disposable acrylic paper palette
Geometric stencil
Repositionable spray adhesive
Copper oil-based stencil paint
Lint-free cloth or paper towels
Satin or gloss spray varnish

1 Pour a pool of Payne's gray acrylic paint onto the palette. Dampen the 1in (2.5cm) glazing brush and blot it on a towel. Base coat the frame and let it dry. Wet the sponge and wring it out until it is just damp. Fill one side with phthalo green paint and pat it on a clean area of the palette to remove any excess. Pat the color over the painted frame, allowing the base coat to show through in places.

2 Pour a small amount of copper metallic paint onto the palette. Fill the clean side of the sponge and pat the copper over the frame in an irregular pattern. For interest, some areas should be more covered than others. Wash paint from the sponge and set aside to dry.

3 Thin phthalo green with a little water and fill the bristles of the round brush with the thinned paint. Holding the brush over the frame, tap gently on the handle to spatter the color. When dry, repeat the process using white paint. Soften harsh spatters by blotting them with a soft cloth. Remove any excess paint from the frame.

4 Spray the star design of the stencil with repositionable spray adhesive. Let it dry until it feels tacky, then blot with a cloth to remove any excess glue. Position in one corner of the frame and with the stencil brush and copper stencil paint, dab color over the stencil. The outer edges of the star should be darkest, with less paint in the center. Reposition the stencil in another corner and repeat until all four corners are done. Let it dry, then mist the finished frame lightly with satin spray varnish. Let this dry, then spray one or two more coats of varnish, allowing each coat to dry thoroughly before applying the next.

METAL FINISHES

USE PURCHASED WOODEN CANDLE HOLDERS OR MAKE YOUR OWN, FOLLOWING THESE SIMPLE DIRECTIONS. FINISH THEM WITH SILVER PAINT AND ENJOY A WONDERFUL CANDLELIT EVENING.

Metallic *Finished* Candlesticks

YOU WILL NEED

10in (25cm) wooden banister spindles
A piece of ½in (1cm) soft pine wood and beading
Saw
Tape measure
Pencil
1in (2.5cm) nail
Wood glue and screws
Hammer
Sandpaper
Tack cloth
½in (1cm) masking tape
Silver metallic paint
Black acrylic paint
1in (2.5cm) flat brush
Paper towel
Yellow ocher acrylic paint (optional)
Satin brush-on varnish

2 Cut a 3in (7.5cm) square base out of the wood. If required for decoration add a border of beading to the edges of the base. Then cut a 3in (7.5cm) circle for the candlestick top. Sand down all pieces and wipe with the tack cloth. Place upright and hammer a nail through the center of the circle (to hold the candle). Fix all three pieces together using masking tape, wood glue, and screws.

4 Use a paper towel to rub away some of the black paint before it is completely dry for a tarnished iron effect. If a rusty look is desired, thin yellow ocher paint with water and dribble a little down the candlestick. Allow to dry, then finish the candlestick with satin varnish.

1 Measure spindle from base to required height (we used 10in/25cm) and draw a line in pencil. Continue line fully around all four sides and cut.

3 When the glue is dry, paint the surface with silver metallic paint. Allow this to dry, then paint over the entire candlestick with black paint.

Fancy Serving Plate

BE THE ENVY OF YOUR GUESTS WHEN YOU SERVE YOUR FAVORITE COOKIES FROM THIS FANCY PLATE. NO ONE WILL GUESS THAT IT IS REALLY PAPIER-MACHE! A LITTLE OF YOUR TIME AND ONLY A FEW SUPPLIES, ARE ALL THAT ARE NEEDED TO CREATE THIS LOVELY ADDITION TO YOUR TABLE.

YOU WILL NEED
Papier-mâché plate
Paper lace doily
Small and large flat brushes
Scissors
Craft glue
Gold foil kit (gold foil, sealer, adhesive, deep brilliant red acrylic paint, brown antiquing paint)
Soft cloth
Black acrylic paint
Non-toxic gloss spray or brush-on varnish

2 Using the base coat color provided in the kit, paint over the doily and the entire plate. Be sure that all areas of the papier-mâché are totally covered. When it is dry, apply a second coat of paint and let it dry thoroughly.

TIP
Always use government certified non-toxic paints and varnishes when you decorate dishes used for food.

4 Cut small pieces of gold foil from the large sheet in the kit. Holding the foil with the shiny side up, press it onto the adhesive. Apply a coat of the sealer over the foil. When dry, brush the antiquing paint over the foiled plate. Wipe away the excess with a soft cloth. Should you wipe away more than you desire, repeat this step. Trim the rim of the plate with a band of black paint. Let it dry completely, then brush several coats of non-toxic gloss varnish over the entire plate, allowing it to dry between coats. When properly finished, this plate can be carefully hand-washed and dried.

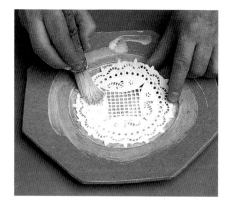

1 With scissors, trim the excess paper from the center design of the doily so it will fit smoothly in the center of the plate. Cover the entire plate with glue thinned slightly with water. While the glue is wet, position the doily and press firmly in place. When completely dry, apply another coat of glue and let it dry.

3 Brush the adhesive included in the kit over the plate. When it is dry, the milky look will disappear and a second coat should then be applied. Let it dry until it is clear and tacky to the touch.

Crackled Foil Wooden egg

THIS LARGE EGG IS EQUALLY BEAUTIFUL LEFT PLAIN OR DECORATED WITH YOUR CHOICE OF PAINTING. DO SEVERAL IN DIFFERENT COLORS OF FOIL AND PLACE THEM IN A BASKET FOR A LOVELY CENTERPIECE.

YOU WILL NEED
Large wooden egg
Silver foil crackle kit (silver foil, crackle medium, sealer, adhesive, black acrylic paint)
½in (1cm) flat brush
A range of acrylic paints
A range of paint brushes
Gloss brush-on or spray varnish

2 Again using the ½in (1cm) brush, apply a coat of adhesive. When it becomes clear, apply another thin, even coat of adhesive and let it dry until the milky look disappears and it feels tacky to the touch.

4 Apply a heavy coat of foil crackle medium over the foiled egg. Set it aside to dry. Cracks will form as the medium dries. Drying times may differ due to temperature and humidity.

1 With the ½in (1cm) brush, seal the wooden egg and let it dry. Paint the egg with the base coat color and let it dry thoroughly. Clean and dry the brush.

TIP
Try this technique on plastic eggs and fill them with goodies for someone special at Easter.

3 Cut or tear the silver foil into smaller pieces and with the shiny side up, use your fingers to press the foil firmly over the egg. The foil will remain on the egg when the paper is lifted.

5 Protect the finish with a coat of sealer or use a gloss spray acrylic varnish. When dry, decorate the egg and then finish with a coat of brush-on or spray varnish, satin or gloss as you prefer.

Verdigris *Plaster Shelf*

This shelf would look smashing in an entryway or sunroom. It only takes a few moments to create this treasure, but no one will know how easy and inexpensive it was to complete.

You will need
Plaster shelf
Verdigris copper foil kit (copper foil, sealer, adhesive, blue-green acrylic paint, blue-green antiquing paint)
½in (1cm) glazing brush
Lint-free paper towels or soft cloth
Satin varnish (optional)

3 Cut the foil into small, easy-to-use pieces. Holding it so the shiny side is up, press the foil firmly over the adhesive. Use a pencil eraser, cotton swab, or the wooden end of a brush to press the foil into the crevices. Allow some of the blue-green base coat to show here and there. Apply a thin coat of sealer over the entire shelf and let it dry completely.

1 Seal the plaster with the sealer provided in the kit. Let it dry. Using the base coat color from the kit and the ½in (1cm) brush, cover the shelf with paint and let it dry.

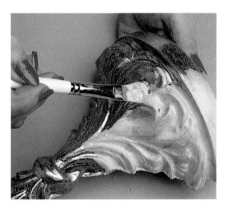

4 Brush the antiquing provided in the kit over the shelf, again being sure to get into the crevices. Let it dry a little before proceeding to the next step.

2 Apply an even coat of the adhesive over the shelf, being careful to get into all crevices. Let it dry until it is no longer a milky color, then apply another coat of adhesive. Set aside to dry until the adhesive is clear and tacky to the touch.

5 Wipe away the antiquing with paper towels or a soft cloth. If you wipe away more than you would like, repeat step 4 and wipe again. Use a damp towel or cloth if the antiquing has become too dry to remove easily. When you are happy with the results, protect the finish by brushing on a coat of sealer or satin varnish.

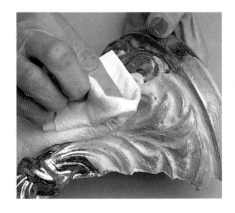

YOU AND YOUR GUESTS ARE SURE TO FEEL LIKE ROYALTY WITH

THIS BEAUTIFULLY DECORATED BOWL ON YOUR SERVING TABLE.

DECORATE THE INDIVIDUAL BOWLS WITH JEWELS OR LEAVE THEM

PLAIN – EITHER WAY THEY ARE SURE TO BE A CONVERSATION PIECE!

Jeweled Bowl

YOU WILL NEED
Wooden bowl set
Gold metallic paint
White, cobalt blue, and phthalo green acrylic paint
1in (2.5cm) glazing brush, ½in (1cm) brush, medium stencil brush
Jewels or glass beads
Craft glue
Matte or satin brush-on or spray varnish
Disposable acrylic paper palette
Lint-free paper towels

1 Base coat the bowl with the gold paint. Be sure to cover it thoroughly. Set aside to dry while you base coat the smaller bowls with the ½in (1cm) brush and gold paint.

2 On a paper palette, place pools of white, cobalt blue, and phthalo green in a triangular shape with the paint almost touching. Pick up some of each color on the stencil brush and blend a little on a clean area of the plate. Working quickly, stipple (pounce) the color over the base color, letting the gold show through here and there. For interest, pick up more of one color as you work. Continue until the entire bowl is covered.

3 As the paint begins to dry but while it is still damp, wipe away some of the color with the paper towel or a soft cloth. On some areas you may need to use more pressure as you rub in order to let the gold show through. This should resemble an old, tarnished gold bowl, so do not rub away too much of the paint.

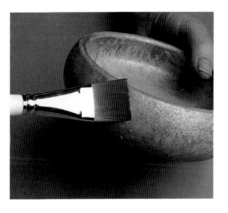

4 Spray or brush on a coat of matte or satin varnish. Let it dry completely, then apply another coat of varnish if desired. Put a drop of glue (about ½ to ¾ the size of the jewel) on the large bowl and press a jewel in place. Hold for a few moments until the glue begins to dry. Repeat this process around the bowl. These bowls can be carefully hand-washed and dried.

Metal Finishes Gallery

Gilded Jewelry Box (above)

This jewelry box has been decorated by adding shells and string with craft glue, and then finishing with paint. The box was base coated with acrylic paint. When dry, gold paint was brushed lightly over the surface.

Crackled Finished Plate (left)

The crackle finish on this serving plate was accomplished by base coating the sealed surface with gold metallic acrylic paint, applying crackle medium in crisscross strokes, and then a top coat of red acrylic paint.

Backgammon Board (right)

The simple paint effect shown here can be used to transform any household object or faded decorative piece. In this case, an old, discarded knife-and-fork case was turned into an attractive backgammon board. The weathered finish was achieved by applying black gloss to a terracotta base paint, using a scrunched-up cloth or tissue. A gold and bronze wax rub was then applied lightly to highlight the playing positions and to enhance the natural texture in the grain of the wood.

Gilt Frame (left)

Picture frames covered in metal leaf or foil make charming accessory pieces. Metal finishes are particularly striking when a complementary color base coat shows through the metallic finish. Here, a base coat of red oxide was applied before the gold paint was added. The surface has then been distressed to allow the base coat to show through.

Verdigris Plate (above)

The natural corrosion of most metals containing copper produces a very distinctive blue-green patina known as verdigris. You can imitate this effect on most surfaces with paints. Here a base coat of turquoise acrylic paint was applied first, and then a coat of gold metallic paint. Then the surface was distressed to allow the turquoise paint to show through.

Verdigris Bowls (left)

The distinctive, mottled green patches of verdigris have been reproduced here with a variety of acrylic paints. Green, turquoise, and blue acrylic paints have been applied to papier-mâché bowls. They have then been embellished with gold paint.

WE ARE
SURROUNDED BY SO
MUCH NATURAL BEAUTY.
THE LOOK AND FEEL OF STONE
FINISHES, SUCH AS MARBLE AND GRANITE,
DELIGHT US, AND WE ARE FASCINATED BY
TORTOISESHELL, ABALONE, AND MOTHER-OF-PEARL FROM
THE OCEAN. USING PAINT, SPONGES, AND EVEN CANDLE SMOKE,
WE ARE ABLE TO REPLICATE MUCH OF NATURE'S SPLENDOR. WITH A

Marble, Stone, and Shell Finishes

LITTLE TIME AND PREPARATION, AND THE PROPER APPLICATION OF PRODUCTS,
YOU WILL HAVE ALL YOU NEED TO PRODUCE MAGNIFICENT WORKS OF ART.
HERE WE HAVE PROVIDED INSTRUCTIONS FOR CREATING MANY
BEAUTIFUL OBJECTS. DIFFERENT TECHNIQUES ARE USED IN
ORDER TO ACHIEVE A REALISTIC-LOOKING MARBLE,
STONE, OR SHELL FINISH, INCLUDING A
UNIQUE "MARBLE" DESIGN. ALL THIS
AND MORE AWAIT YOU IN THIS
EXCITING CHAPTER.

PUT YOUR FAVORITE PHOTO IN THIS FAUX MALACHITE PICTURE FRAME AND IT IS SURE TO BE A CONVERSATION PIECE.

Foiled *Malachite Picture Frame*

YOU WILL NEED
Picture frame
Sandpaper
Soft lint-free cloth
Phthalo green, viridian, permanent sap green, and black acrylic paints
½in (1cm) brush, large shader, medium round brush
Disposable acrylic paper palette
Paper towels
Gold foil kit (gold foil, sealer, adhesive, deep brilliant red acrylic paint, brown antiquing paint)
Satin or gloss spray or brush-on varnish

2 Paint circles loosely in the wet paint with the dirty brush loaded with phthalo green. Both shades of green should be visible when the circles are completed. Thin the black paint with a little water so it will flow easily. With irregular strokes, outline some areas of the circles.

4 With the round brush, apply the adhesive in a hit-and-miss fashion around the circles and on some of the wavy lines between the circles. Let it dry until it is clear and tacky, then apply another coat and let it dry until it is no longer milky. It will be very sticky.

1 Sand the frame and wipe with a soft cloth. Dampen the brush and blot on paper towel to remove excess water. Pool some phthalo green onto the palette and with the ½in (1cm) brush, apply the base coat. Allow to dry. Fill the shader brush with viridian and paint over the base coat, with strokes going in different directions. While the paint is wet, go to step 2.

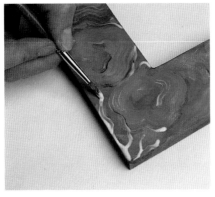

3 Paint some wavy lines between the circles with viridian. Soften them with the dry shader brush and let them dry.

5 With the shiny side of the foil up, press pieces of foil over the glue. When the paper is lifted, the foil will remain on the frame. When this is completed, brush the sealer over the entire frame. Protect the painting by brushing or spraying a coat of satin or gloss varnish over the frame.

Marbled Papier-Mâché Boxes

ARE YOU LOOKING FOR A QUICK AND EASY GIFT BOX OR DECORATIVE ITEM FOR YOUR HOME? LEAVE PLAIN OR DECORATE AS YOU WISH, AND IN LESS THAN AN HOUR YOU CAN COMPLETE THESE BEAUTIFUL BOXES.

YOU WILL NEED
Papier-mâché boxes in assorted
shapes and sizes
Bergundy water-based spray paint
Silver and copper water-based
highlight spray paint
Waxed paper plate
Paper towels
Copper foil crackle kit (copper foil,
sealer, adhesive, crackle medium,
dark gray-green acrylic paint)
Large shader (or flat) brush
Satin or gloss spray or brush-on
varnish
Silver glitter spray

1 Spray the box inside and out with bergundy spray paint. Papier-mâché absorbs paint quickly, so if the coverage is spotty, apply a second coat after the first one is completely dry.

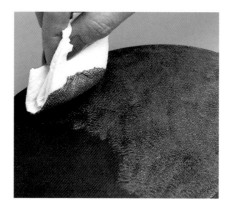

2 Spray a small amount of copper highlight spray paint on the paper plate. Fold a paper towel into a small square and pat the color over the box. Try to avoid hard edges. If you prefer, spray the copper highlight spray paint over the box and, while it is wet, pat with a paper towel. If a towel with a design is used, you will achieve a lacy effect. Let this dry completely.

TIP . . .
Protect the area by spreading old newspapers or a sheet of plastic over the table and spraying into a large cardboard box.

---

3 Apply a coat of adhesive to the rim of the box using the shader brush. Let it dry until it is no longer milky in color, then apply another coat and let it dry until it is clear and tacky to the touch. Cut pieces of copper foil, shiny side up, and with firm pressure apply foil over the adhesive. Press small pieces of copper foil over any areas on the rim that are not covered.

4 Brush the crackle medium over the foiled area and set aside to dry. As the medium dries, cracks will begin to appear in the foil. When the piece is thoroughly dry, brush on a coat of the sealer or varnish to protect the finish. If desired, line the inside of the box with fabric of your choice. The blue box was sprayed with bergundy water-based paint, then sprayed with silver highlight spray paint, patted with a towel, and finally sprayed lightly with silver glitter.

Fantasy Marbled Table

This table would add a lovely accent to a sunroom or patio. Finish with outdoor varnish and it would be serviceable as well as decorative. You might want to make a matching shelf or clock.

You will need
Small table
Sandpaper
Wood sealer
Permanent sap green, purple, ivory, and turquoise green acrylic paints
1in (2.5cm) glazing brush, large shader (or flat) brush, small script liner
Fine-pore synthetic sponge
½in (1cm) masking tape
Copper foil kit (copper foil, sealer, adhesive, crackle medium, dark gray-green acrylic paint)
Patina gel
Lint-free cloth
Varnish

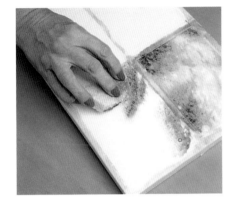

1 Sand and seal the entire table. When dry, lightly sand again and wipe away the residue. Divide the table top into four equal sections with ½in (1cm) masking tape, and tape along the edge of the table using the full width of the tape. Press the tape firmly. Base coat the table top with ivory. While this dries, paint the sides and legs of the table with permanent sap green. Wet the table top with water. Pick up permanent sap green on a damp sponge, and lightly pat in drifts of color diagonally from top to bottom of each sectioned area. Moving the table top around causes the color to float in the desired direction.

2 Use the liner brush to create squiggly veins while the paint is wet. The more irregular the lines, the more realistic the veins. As the paint begins to dry, soften the vein lines with a soft brush or the edge of the sponge and let it dry.

3 Repeat step 1, using each of the following colors; purple, turquoise green, and ivory. Stroke in a few veins (as in step 2) with one or two of these colors. Allow each addition of color to dry before going to the next. If you find that you have too much color in one area, sponge on a bit of ivory here and there.

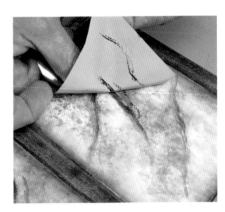

4 Remove the tape and paint the lines and border with permanent sap green. Apply adhesive over the border. Use the liner to apply adhesive over some of the vein lines. When it no longer looks milky, press copper foil over the adhesive, shiny side up. Use the sealer, or brush on varnish, over the foil sections. Antique the foil areas with patina gel. Wipe away any excess. As the paint begins to dry, soften the vein lines with a soft brush or the lint-free cloth. When dry, use gloss varnish to protect the surface.

Granite *Pedestal*

NO ONE WILL BELIEVE THIS LITTLE PEDESTAL IS REALLY PAPIER-MÂCHÉ! FOR A REALLY DRAMATIC EFFECT, PLACE A FAVORITE PLANT ON IT AND LET THE HANGING FOLIAGE ECHO THE STENCILED INLAYS.

YOU WILL NEED
Small papier-mâché pedestal
Pale gray, black,
and white acrylic paint
2in (5cm) and 1in (2.5cm) flat brush,
1in (2.5cm) stencil brush
Fine-pore sea sponge
Paper towel
Disposable acrylic paper palette
Spray or brush-on gloss varnish
½in (1cm) masking tape
Ivy or leaf stencil

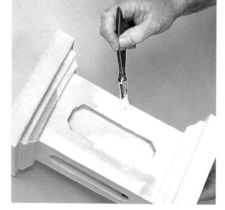

1 Paint the pedestal with the 2in (5cm) brush and the pale gray paint. (If desired, black and white can be mixed to a pale gray – just be sure to mix enough for the entire pedestal and store the remaining paint in a plastic film canister for touch-ups.) Let the paint dry completely.

2 Pour a puddle of black paint onto the palette and pick up some of the paint with a damp sponge. Blot on a paper towel to remove the excess paint and lightly stipple (pounce) the color over the pedestal. Let this dry completely.

3 Pick up some white paint with the stiff bristle brush or an old toothbrush, and spatter randomly over the entire surface. Again, leave to dry.

4 Brush or spray a *light* coat of varnish over the pedestal to seal it. Allow this to dry thoroughly.

5 On the top of the pedestal form a square by pressing a strip of masking tape ½in (1cm) from the edges. Press a second strip ¼in (5mm) to the inside of the first strip. Press firmly along the edges of the tape for a good seal. Repeat this process on the base of the pedestal.

7 Place the stencil in the recessed area of the pedestal and, holding it firmly in place, stencil over the design with the stencil brush and black paint. Be sure to blot the brush on a dry paper towel to remove excess paint and use a pouncing motion in order to prevent bleed out under the stencil. Repeat this on the three remaining sides and allow to dry.

6 With the 1in (2.5cm) brush, apply a coat of black paint between the strips of tape on the top of the pedestal and on the base. Remove the tape carefully as soon as the paint has dried.

8 Remove the stencil carefully and then varnish the entire pedestal with several coats of varnish, allowing drying time between applications. It is important that a gloss varnish be used as granite is polished and has a high luster.

YOU WILL NEED
Wooden fan-shaped box
Sandpaper
Wood sealer
Tack cloth
Paper towels
Disposable acrylic paper palette
1in (2.5cm) brush, small flat shader
Light ivory or black acrylic paint
Gold metallic paint
Mother-of-pearl and abalone kit (pearlized
and abalone foil, ivory and black acrylic
paint, sealer, adhesive)
Gloss varnish

Fan Keepsake Box

THESE WONDERFUL BOXES ARE NOT ONLY PERFECT AS KEEPSAKE BOXES, BUT THEY WOULD MAKE A WONDERFUL GIFT FOR A PIECE OF JEWELRY. COVERED WITH IRIDESCENT FOIL, THE BOX LOOKS LIKE ABALONE SHELL WHEN BASE COATED WITH BLACK OR MOTHER-OF-PEARL WHEN BASE COATED WITH LIGHT IVORY.

1 Sand the entire box, apply a coat of sealer with the 1in (2.5cm) brush, and when dry, lightly sand again. Wipe the surface with the tack cloth to remove the sanding dust. For the abalone finish, base coat the box with black paint, again using the 1in (2.5cm) brush. Use light ivory paint if you want a mother-of-pearl surface. Clean and dry the brush.

2 Then apply the adhesive in a thin, even coat. Let it dry until it is no longer milky-looking, then apply another coat of adhesive and let it dry until it is clear and tacky to the touch.

3 Cut the foil into small, easy-to-use pieces. Holding it so the shiny side is up, press it firmly onto the surface with your fingers. Lift off the clear backing paper, leaving the mother-of-pearl or the abalone finish on the box. Repeat until the entire outside surface of the box is covered.

4 With the flat shader brush, trim the edges with gold paint. When it is dry, apply the sealer or gloss varnish and let it dry.

TIP
Try this technique on other hard surfaces such as plaster, bisque, ceramic, plastic, and glass.

Smoked Marble Fireplace Screen

A LOOK OF ELEGANT MARBLE IS QUICK AND EASY TO ACHIEVE WITH THIS SURPRISE TECHNIQUE. REPEAT THE MARBLING THE OTHER SIDE OF THE SCREEN OR PAINT A DESIGN.

YOU WILL NEED
Small wooden fireplace screen
Candle
Old table knife
Matches
Light ivory and black acrylic paints
Light brown gel stain
Old paintbrush or old toothbrush
Lint-free paper towels or soft cloth
1in (2.5cm) glazing brush, medium shader (or flat) brush
Chalk or pencil
Craft glue
Gold foil
Gold metallic paint
Brush-on or spray gloss varnish

1 With chalk or pencil mark a border 2in (5cm) from the outer edge of the screen, as a guide for the border design. Stain the border with light brown gel and let dry. Pour a small amount of black paint on the palette and thin it to an inky consistency with water. Fill the bristles of an old brush or toothbrush with paint and spatter the stained area.

2 Mix a little black into light ivory for a slightly gray tint and base coat the wood inside the border. When dry, lightly sand, wipe away the residue and apply another coat of paint. When dry, lightly varnish the entire screen and let it dry.

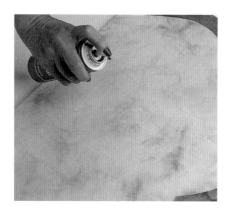

3 Light the candle and have someone hold the knife so a thin, steady wisp of smoke floats from the flame of the candle. Hold the screen over the smoke, moving it so it forms a marble pattern on the painted area. Continue until you have the desired amount of marbling. If you are not happy with your results the first time, remove the smoke pattern with a little soapy water. Dry and repeat the process. Clean the smoke from the stained area. Lightly spray with varnish.

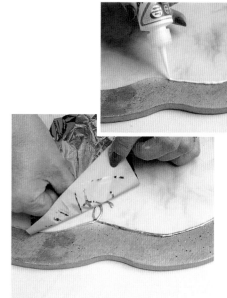

4 Place a bead of glue around the board where the stain and marbled area touch. Let dry until clear. Cut the gold foil into small, easy-to-use pieces. Shiny side up, press the foil firmly onto the bead of glue, covering it completely. With the shader brush and gold paint, trim the edges of the fireplace screen. When all painting is dry, spray several coats of gloss varnish over the screen, drying thoroughly between coats.

84

MARBLE, STONE, AND SHELL FINISHES

Granite Serving Tray

YOU WILL FIND THIS BEAUTIFUL TRAY IS NOT ONLY USEFUL FOR SERVING BUT ALSO LOVELY AS A HOLDER FOR FRUIT, VEGETABLES, OR FLOWERS ON YOUR DINING TABLE.

1 Prepare the wood by sanding and sealing the tray. When the seal is dry, lightly sand again and wipe away the dust with a tack cloth. Base coat with viridian using the ½in (1cm) brush.

2 Mask off the inner sides and ends of the tray. With a wet but not dripping sponge, pat dark olive green over the inside bottom of the tray. Be sure to let some of the base coat show through and turn the sponge as you work to avoid a repetitive pattern. With a clean, damp sponge, pat mid-green over the dark olive green. Be sure that the base coat and the dark olive green show through and remember to turn the sponge as you work. Let it dry.

3 Place two rows of masking tape ¼in (5mm) apart around the bottom and sides of the tray and press firmly for a good seal. Repeat along the edges of the tray. Use the shader brush and gold paint to fill in the areas between the two rows of tape. Use two coats if necessary. Remove the tape immediately upon finishing the trim. If there is any bleeding of the gold onto the base color, clean up by painting over it with viridian.

4 Carefully paint gold inside the handle cutouts on the ends of the tray. Let them dry, then apply a second coat of the gold paint.

5 Finish with a coat of brush-on or spray varnish. When it is dry, repeat until you achieve the desired finish, drying thoroughly between each application.

MARBLE, STONE, AND SHELL FINISHES

Tortoiseshell *Planter*

WHILE THIS WAS ORIGINALLY DESIGNED AS A PLANTER, IT COULD JUST AS EASILY SERVE AS A DECORATIVE WASTEBASKET. THIS BEAUTIFUL PROJECT WILL INTRIGUE AND DELIGHT ALL WHO SEE IT!

YOU WILL NEED
Wooden planter
Fine sandpaper
Tack cloth
Black acrylic paint
3in (7.5cm), 2in (5cm), and 1in (2.5cm) flat brush
¼in (5mm) masking tape
Red iron oxide, raw sienna, and black acrylic paint
Clear acrylic retarder
Permanent gold marking pen
Ruler
Spray or brush-on varnish
Gold stencil paint
Soft cloth or paper towel

1 Sand the entire planter with the fine sandpaper and wipe away the sanding dust with the tack cloth. Base coat the planter (inside and out) with black paint and allow to dry completely. On each of the four sides, lay a strip of masking tape along each edge, and two diagonal strips, from corner to corner, as shown.

2 With the 3in (7.5cm) brush paint the outside of the planter with red iron oxide paint and allow this to dry.

MARBLE, STONE, AND SHELL FINISHES

3 Working on one side at a time, brush on a coat of acrylic retarder and proceed to step 4 immediately.

5 Carefully drag either the 2in (5cm) or the 3in (7.5cm) brush across the planter in a diagonal direction to create the tortoiseshell effect. Working quicky, repeat this process (continuing to brush in the same diagonal direction) until the one side is completed. Leave the paint to dry, then continue in this manner until all four sides are completed.

4 With the 1in (2.5cm) brush, place squiggles of raw sienna and a few random dots of black paint to the wet side of the planter. Go to step 5 without delay.

6 As soon as the paint on each side is dry, carefully remove the tape to expose the black stripes. Apply one coat of varnish and allow it to dry.

7 With the permanent gold marking pen, and using a ruler as a guide, carefully outline the exposed black tape lines.

9 Brush or spray on several coats of varnish, allowing drying time between each application.

8 Gently remove the "shine" around the top edge and base of the planter with fine grade sandpaper and wipe with the tack cloth. Using a soft cloth or paper towel, rub gold stencil paint over both these edges and allow to dry.

Marble, Stone, and Shell Finishes Gallery

Green Marble Fireplace (above)
Notice the color variation in this detail. You should strive to have a visible variety of greens, and should be careful not to let the veining pattern be too distracting.

White Marble Fireplace (left)
Marble effects are achieved by using a variety of equipment for painting – a toothbrush, plastic wrap for scumbling, a feather to apply the white veins, and a fine, artist's brush for detailed work. Seeing through the finish to the base coat adds the illusion of depth to the surface.

Stone-effect Picture Frames (below)
Try using natural objects such as shells to enhance stone paint effects. These frames were base coated with cream acrylic paint on the right and peach acrylic paint on the left. Diluted gold paint was then brushed lightly over the surface.

92

Candle Box (right)

A combination of techniques has been used on this candle box. After base coating, the lid and plinth were marbled. Decorative stroke work and trim were added with gold metallic acrylic paint. A floral picture, decoupaged in the insert, and a coat of varnish completed the project.

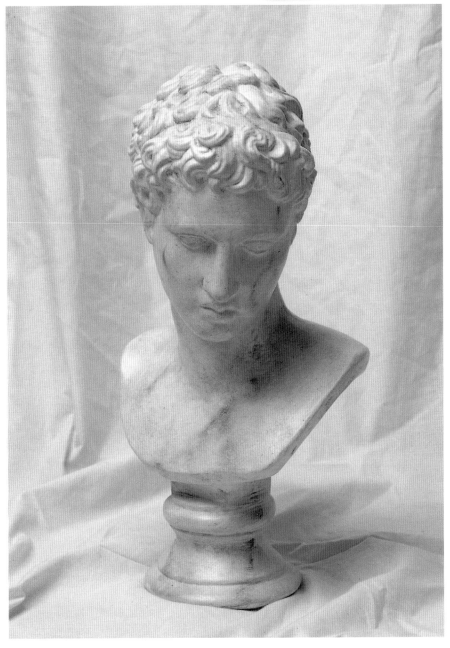

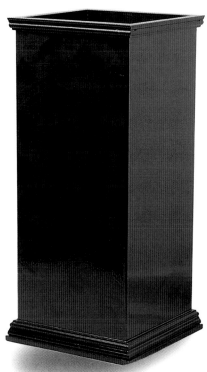

93

Tortoiseshell Umbrella Stand (above)

Tortoiseshell was frequently used by the Victorians to decorate a whole range of household items. It is possible to achieve a realistic copy using only paints and varnishes. Here, a natural-red base color is used, but a strong yellow is just as attractive.

Marbled Plaster Bust (left)

This marbled plaster bust is finished in a gray-marble effect to imitate a grand sculpture from an earlier age. When imitating marble, it is always useful to have either a real sample or a photograph of the original.

DID YOU EVER
WALK INTO A ROOM
AND NOTICE THAT IT WAS
LACKING A WARM, LIVED-IN FEELING?
ACCESSORIES AND DECORATIVE TOUCHES
SAY SO MUCH ABOUT THE PERSONALITY OF THE
RESIDENT, AND MAKE A DEFINITE STATEMENT TO THOSE
VISITING THE PREMISES. WITH A FEW SUPPLIES AND A LITTLE
IMAGINATION IT IS POSSIBLE TO TURN EVEN THE MUNDANE INTO THE

Decorative Finishes

EXTRAORDINARY. JUST TAKE A FEW MOMENTS TO LOOK AROUND YOU AND ENVISION THE POSSIBLE
CHANGES IN ONE ROOM, THEN BEGIN TO THINK OF HOW YOU CAN BRING ABOUT THOSE CHANGES.
EVERYONE HAS POSSESSIONS THAT CAN BE UPDATED WITH LITTLE EFFORT. THE OLD FRAME
IN THE ATTIC, A DISCOLORED LAMPSHADE, PERHAPS AN OLD WASTEBASKET OR A
FLOWER POT COULD BE GIVEN A FACELIFT AND A NEW LIFE. WITH THE
DECORATIVE FINISH PRODUCTS AVAILABLE AND MANY INNOVATIVE
METHODS FOR THEIR USE, YOU CAN LITERALLY CREATE A NEW
LOOK FROM THE OLD IN A MATTER OF A FEW HOURS.
YOU WILL FIND MANY FANTASTIC IDEAS INCLUDED
IN THIS CHAPTER, AND NO DOUBT YOU
WILL THINK OF MANY EXCITING
WAYS TO ADAPT THEM TO
YOUR OWN USE.

Faux *Finish* Picture *Frame*

PAPIER-MACHE COMES IN SO MANY INTERESTING SHAPES AND SIZES. WHEN IT IS PROPERLY FINISHED, IT CAN BE QUITE LOVELY, AS THIS FRAME, WHICH IS PERFECT FOR YOUR FAVORITE PHOTO OR A MIRROR, SHOWS.

YOU WILL NEED
Papier-mâché picture frame
Sealer
Gold metallic paint
Crackle medium
Red oxide and black acrylic paint
1in (2.5cm) flat brush, small round
brush or liner
½in (1cm) masking tape
Cherub stencil
Repositionable spray adhesive
Gold stencil oil-based paint
Soft lint-free cloth
Brush-on or spray varnish

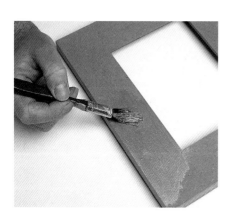

1 Seal the frame with sealer, and let it dry completely. Base coat the entire frame with the gold metallic paint and let it dry thoroughly, then brush on a heavy, even coat of crackle medium. Allow this to dry until it feels tacky when touched.

2 Quickly brush black paint in one direction *only* over the medium. As the paint begins to dry, cracks will form in the top coat, and the gold base coat will show through the cracks.

3 For an easy-to-paint border, place a row of masking tape ¼in (5mm) from the edge of the frame. A second row of tape is placed ¼in (5mm) from the first row. Press the edges of the tape firmly to form a good seal.

4 Using the red paint and a small flat brush, paint the area between the two pieces of tape.

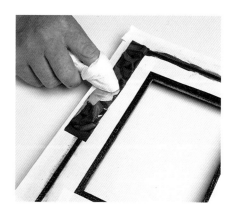

5 Spray the back of the stencil with the spray adhesive. When it feels sticky, position the stencil in the center of the frame. Rub gold stencil paint over the stencil using a soft cloth. Rub a light layer of gold over the red stripe. Remove the tape, and when the gold is dry, finish by brushing a coat of sealer over the frame or use a spray varnish.

Country Flatware Tray

WHETHER YOU ARE TAKING THIS HANDY TRAY TO A PICNIC OR SIMPLY USING IT AT THE BARBECUE, IT IS SURE TO BE ONE OF YOUR MOST-USED ITEMS.

YOU WILL NEED
Wooden flatware tray, unfinished
¼in (5mm) masking tape
Navy blue pickling gel
Lint-free paper towels or soft cloth
Tracing paper
Pen or pencil
Transfer paper
Stylus
Wood resist or masking fluid
Cadmium yellow deep and cobalt blue acrylic paint
1in (2.5cm) glazing brush
Sandpaper
Satin spray or brush-on varnish

1 Brush on or wipe pickling gel over the entire tray. Rub it into the wood and wipe away any excess. The gel will cause the grain of the wood to show through. When the tray is completely dry, place a row of ¼in (5mm) masking tape ¼in (5mm) from the top edge of the tray. Press firmly along the edge of the tape with the fingers for a good seal. Paint can be applied over the tape, which will be left on until the painting is completed.

2 Paint the entire tray with cobalt blue. While the paint dries, trace the design onto tracing paper. Transfer it to the dry tray using the transfer paper and stylus. Draw around the design with wood resist or masking fluid. If using wood resist try to draw just outside the lines so they can be erased later. Masking fluid can be placed directly on the lines as it will be peeled off when painting is finished. Either product must dry before you proceed to step 3.

3 With the large brush, streak a coat of the cadmium yellow deep paint over the dark blue paint. Be sure to not cover it completely as much of this color will be removed later.

4 When the tray is completely dry, remove the tape. If masking fluid was used, peel it away at this time. Erase all transfer lines if wood resist was used.

5 Sand the tray to remove some of the yellow paint. The tray should look old and well-used when it is finished, so some areas should be sanded more than others. Finish with satin spray or brush-on varnish. The tray should resemble an antique, so a shiny finish should not be used. Be sure to allow adequate drying time before applications of varnish.

Blanket Box

THE STORAGE OF BLANKETS IN THE SUMMER

TIME IS ALWAYS A PROBLEM, BUT THE PROBLEM IS SOLVED WITH THIS

IMPRESSIVE BLANKET BOX THAT CAN ALSO DOUBLE AS A BENCH.

YOU WILL NEED
Wooden box
Pale cream and black acrylic paint
2in (5cm), 1in (2.5cm), and ½in
(1cm) flat brush, ½in (1cm)
stencil brush
½in (1cm) masking tape
Victorian corner stencil
Gold foil kit (adhesive, gold foil,
brown antiquing gel)
Soft, lint-free cloth and paper towel
Scissors
Photocopy of acanthus leaves
(or similar leaf or scroll work)
Craft glue
Bristle brush or old toothbrush
Satin or gloss, spray or
brush-on varnish

1 Using the 1in (5cm) brush and pale cream, base coat the entire box and allow to dry. Trim the base plinth and the top edge with black and let this dry before proceeding to the next step.

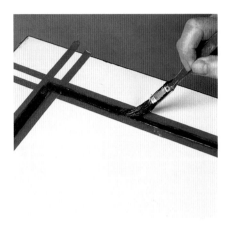

2 Along the top, front, and two sides of the box, press masking tape 3in (7.5cm) from the edge. A second row of tape is then placed ½in (1cm) inside the first row. Press the edges of the tape firmly for a good seal, then paint between the strips with black paint. Remove the tape carefully as soon as the paint is dry.

4 Press masking tape over the black stripes and brush the foil adhesive over each rectangle as shown in the photo. Be sure to read and follow the directions on the adhesive label.

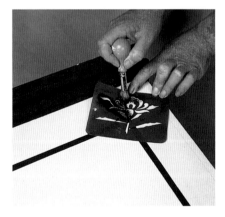

5 Press the gold foil over the adhesive, keeping the shiny side up. (Again, read and follow the instructions on the packaging.) When all areas have been foiled, carefully remove the tape and lightly varnish the entire box and allow to dry.

3 Holding the stencil firmly in place at one corner of the top, stencil the design using the black paint and the stencil brush. Be sure to blot the brush on a dry paper towel to remove the excess paint, and stipple (pounce) the paint over the design to eliminate bleed out. Repeat this process on all four corners of the top, front, and two sides.

6 With scissors, carefully cut out the photocopied designs and arrange them on the top of the box. Move them around until you are pleased with the effect.

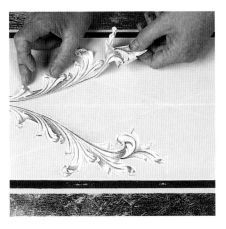

7 Working one section at a time, brush an even coat of glue on the back of one of the cutouts and press it in place. Gently rub to remove any air bubbles. Continue until all pieces have been glued, then set aside to dry completely.

8 Seal the glued cutouts with a light coat of varnish, being careful to cover all edges, and allow to dry. With the soft, lint-free cloth, apply the antiquing gel over the box and rub away the excess with a clean area of the cloth. Let this dry, then if more antiquing is desired, repeat the process and again, allow to dry.

9 Thin a little black paint with water to an inky consistency. Using the bristle brush or old toothbrush, spatter the box to create age specks. When the spatters are dry apply several coats of varnish, allowing drying time between each application.

T URN A PLAIN LAMPSHADE INTO A FASHION STATEMENT. PAINT IT WITH THE COLORS USED HERE OR CHOOSE OTHERS TO HARMONIZE WITH THE REST OF YOUR FURNISHINGS.

Decorative Lampshade

1 Trace the pattern on tracing paper and transfer it to the lamp-shade using transfer paper or draw the design freehand using a soft pencil. Space the design evenly around the shade.

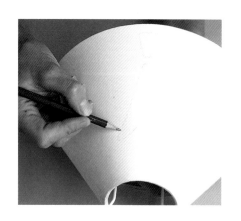

DECORATIVE FINISHES

2 With the craft knife carefully cut along the lines of the triangular shapes above and below the tulips. You may find it helpful to hold a small piece of wood under the shade as you cut.

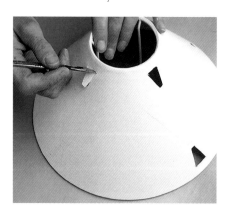

TIP

Try using stencils to create other cutout lampshade designs.

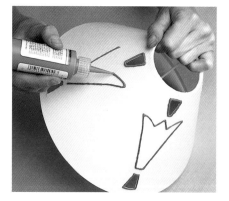

3 Using the green shiny fabric paint, draw around the design and along the edges of the cutout areas, applying steady pressure to the bottle as you work. Allow this paint to dry thoroughly – drying time will vary due to temperature and humidity – then with the round brush, paint the tulips with red fabric paint. When dry, apply a second coat for good coverage.

YOU WILL NEED
Lamp with plain fabric shade
Tracing paper
Transfer paper
Pen or pencil
Stylus
Craft knife
Dark blue, red, and lemon yellow acrylic fabric paint
Green shiny fabric paint
Disposable acrylic paper palette
Medium round brush
Small-pore synthetic sponge

4 Thin the blue fabric paint to an inky consistency with water. Fill the bristles of the round brush with this mixture and tap gently on the handle to spatter paint over the shade. Pour a pool of yellow fabric paint on the palette. Wet the sponge and wring out the excess water. With the damp sponge, pat color over the shade. Soften any harsh edges with the edge of the sponge.

Textured Letter Holder

A PLACE FOR EVERYTHING AND EVERYTHING IN ITS PLACE GOES THE OLD SAYING. THIS LETTER HOLDER WILL BE USEFUL FOR THOSE DREADED FIRST-OF-THE-MONTH BILLS AS WELL AS FOR OTHER REMINDERS, AND CARDS AND LETTERS CONVEYING GOOD WISHES.

YOU WILL NEED
Letter holder
Medium-grain sand
Craft glue
Cobalt blue and white acrylic paints
Red copper metallic paint
½in (1cm) glazing brush,
Medium round brush
Mixing knife (optional)
Tracing paper
Transfer paper
Disposable acrylic paper palette
Pen or pencil
Stylus
Satin spray varnish

2 With the mixing knife, mix equal parts of sand and glue on the paper palette. Add cobalt blue and mix well. Brush the sand/ glue/paint mixture over the surface, being careful to keep out of the border around the designs. Set aside to dry. Clean your brush thoroughly, carefully removing all traces of the glue/paint mixture.

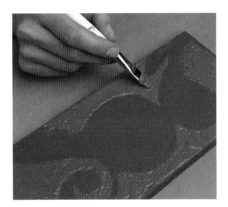

4 Paint the border around the designs with white paint. Use a clean, dry brush to smudge the white paint into the area around the starfish. If necessary, add a little water to the brush and soften any harsh areas. When dry, any necessary touch-ups can be made using the correct colors. When all paint is dry, finish with a spray varnish.

1 Base coat the letter holder with cobalt blue. Set aside to dry and trace the design on the tracing paper using a pen or pencil. When the letter holder is dry, use the transfer paper and stylus to transfer the design onto it.

3 Lightly dry brush over the texture design with red copper metallic paint. The sand will cause the paint to adhere to the texture and will allow some of the base color to show through.

THIS RUSTIC-LOOKING DECORATED CHOPPING

BOARD WOULD ENHANCE ANY KITCHEN, BE

IT MODERN OR TRADITIONAL.

Decorated
Chopping Board

1 Sand the chopping board and wipe away the residue with the tack cloth. Make a wash of color by mixing a little of the medium green paint with water until it is of an inky consistency. Brush this mixture over one side of the board.

2 From a magazine, wallpaper etc., cut out colored pictures which co-ordinate with your decor. Carefully trim away the excess paper. Arrange the cutouts on the board in a pleasing pattern. With the 1in (2.5cm) brush, apply an even coat of craft glue to the back of one picture and use your fingers to press it in place. Glue each picture in the same manner, then gently rub across them several times in different directions to remove any air bubbles. Set aside to dry.

3 Using the 2in (5cm) brush and vertical strokes, apply an even coat of glue over the top of the board and let this dry, then repeat with horizontal strokes and let dry. Brush on a thin, even coat of crackle medium and allow it to dry until it is very tacky, then brush a coat of satin varnish over the medium. Cracks will form during the drying time.

YOU WILL NEED
Wooden chopping board
Sandpaper
Tack cloth
Medium green acrylic paint
2in (5cm) and 1in (2.5cm) flat brush
Colored pictures from magazines
Scissors
White craft glue
Two-part crackle medium
Light brown gel stain
Paper towel or soft cloth
Spray or brush-on satin varnish
Ribbon (optional)

4 Rub the light brown gel stain into the cracks with a paper towel or soft cloth and wipe away any excess. Allow this to dry thoroughly, then spray or brush on a coat of satin varnish. If desired, a ribbon can be added for decoration.

108

DECORATIVE FINISHES

Embossed
Nursery Mobile

YOUR BABY WILL SPEND MANY HAPPY AND PEACEFUL HOURS WATCHING THIS MOBILE TURN IN THE BREEZE. IT IS SO CUTE AND EASY TO MAKE THAT YOU WILL WANT TO DO SEVERAL AS GIFTS.

YOU WILL NEED
4 sheets of medium-weight cardboard
4 sheets of matching or contrasting marbled paper
Animal stencil
Stylus
Burnishing tool (or knitting needle)
Craft glue
Soft cloth
Top coat (optional)
Hole punch
Royal blue, yellow ocher, dusty rose, and orange oil-based stencil paint
5 lengths of medium-weight florist wire
1½ yards (1.4m) of nylon cord or kite string

2 Center the stencil over the smaller circle and outline the design using the small end of the stylus. Repeat until all animals are traced. Using the burnishing tool or the head of a knitting needle, emboss each animal within the lines of the design.

3 Fold the cloth into a small, smooth square and use it to apply the stencil paint over the embossed area. Allow to dry. Glue the painted circle off-center on the larger circle and set aside to dry. Make a hanger by twisting two pieces of florist wire together. Repeat this process and attach the two hangers together by twisting the remaining wire to the center of each hanger. Tie cords or strings of different lengths to the circles and attach them to the hangers.

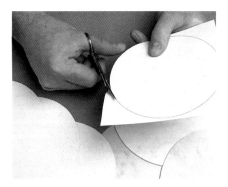

1 Cut four 6in (15cm) circles from the marbled paper. From the cardboard, cut four 4½in (11.5cm) circles.

Jewelry Box With Austrian Flowers

A SPECIAL LOADING AND PAINTING TECHNIQUE IS NECESSARY FOR COMPLETING THE DESIGN ON THIS BOX. PRACTICE PAINTING BEFORE YOU BEGIN YOUR PROJECT.

YOU WILL NEED
Wooden jewelry box
Sandpaper
Wood sealer
Tack cloth
Acrylic retarder
Dark portrait pink, mid-olive green, mid-pink, mid-maroon, yellow oxide, maroon, ultramarine, light ivory, dark olive green, cobalt blue, light portrait pink, and mid-green acrylic paints
1in (2.5cm) glazing brush, large filbert brush, medium flat brush, medium round brush
Glass jar
Satin brush-on or spray varnish
Disposable acrylic paper palette
Paper towels
Tracing paper and graphite paper
Pencil or pen
Eraser
Stylus
Old brush or old toothbrush

1 Sand, seal, let dry, and sand again lightly. Wipe away the sanding residue with the tack cloth. Base coat the entire jewelry box with dark portrait pink, using the 1in (2.5cm) brush. Let the paint dry thoroughly.

4 Working on the color corner of the brush, apply the dark olive green paint in random "squiggles" in one area of the box top.

2 Clean and blot the brush on a paper towel. Fill the bristles with acrylic retarder and brush this over the top of the box. Working quickly, pick up a little dark portrait pink and blend the paint through the bristles by working back and forth on the palette.

5 Wipe the brush with the paper towel to remove any excess paint. With the bristles flat against the wood, use gentle crisscross strokes to soften any hard edges. Apply this color here and there, blending well; then clean the brush and blot it on a paper towel.

3 On the corner of the dirty brush, pick up a little dark olive green. Blend the colors slightly by pressing the full width of the brush onto the palette and making a few small strokes in the same place.

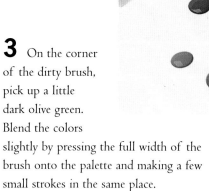

6 Repeat the process, picking up maroon, then again using ultramarine. If the surface begins to dry before you finish, let it dry completely, re-apply the acrylic retarder and continue as before. Paint the entire box in this manner and set it aside to dry.

7 Using an old brush or tooth-brush, spatter the box with ultramarine thinned with water to an inky consistency. Test the consistency of the paint first by spattering on a piece of paper or on a scrap of wood before going to the project.

8 Trace the floral design on tracing paper, then transfer the pattern to the lid of the box using the stylus and graphite paper. Use light pressure so the lines will be just dark enough to be visible.

9 The flowers and leaves are painted with the medium round brush. Wet the brush and tap it several times on the side of the jar to remove excess water. Do not towel blot. Completely fill the bristles with mid-green. Holding the brush as horizontal to the palette as possible, drag one side through dark olive green. When properly loaded and held at eye level, the brush load should look like a finger and a fingernail. Don't skimp on paint or this technique will not work.

10 Holding the brush so the mid-green is slightly to the side, paint the leaf. You can begin at the tip and apply pressure as you pull downward toward the center, or begin with pressure at the bottom of the leaf and use less pressure as you pull upward toward the tip. Vary some of the leaves by adding a touch of cobalt blue or any of the pink shades to the light load on the brush. For the flips, load only with dark olive green and drag through light ivory. Hold the brush with the light side toward the inside of the leaf and paint the stroke with little pressure, more pressure, then little pressure as you follow the outer curve of the leaf.

11 Rinse the brush by swishing it through clean water, then load the brush as in step 9 with mid-pink, dragging one side through mid-maroon, then through light ivory. Remember that for a proper load, the brush must be almost horizontal to the palette.

15 Pull downward following the curve of the petal. When done properly, all three colors will be seen and the petal will be beautifully streaked. Continue in this manner until the bowl of the rose is completed.

12 With the mid-pink side next to the palette, heel into maroon. Beginning in the center of the rose bowl, set the brush dark side down, and mash to spread the bristles. Continue in this manner, following the shape of the bowl until one side of the bowl is filled with color. Then repeat on the other side.

13 Fill the bristles of the brush with mid-pink. Drag one side through mid-maroon and the other side through light ivory.
Dribble light ivory along the top of the first petal by holding the brush with this color to the top and slightly to the side. The more irregular the dribbles are, the prettier your flowers will be.

16 For the outer petals, load the brush as in step 13. Dribble the light ivory along the outside edge of one petal, then mash the bristles and push into the dribbled edge. Use less pressure as you move toward completion. Remember to follow the curve of the petal and to keep the light ivory side facing up as you paint.

17 Following the instructions in step 16, paint as many petals on the rose as you desire. You may find it best to allow one row of petals to dry before painting the next row. Should a mistake be made, it is easy to wipe away without ruining the previous layer of painting.

14 Turn the brush so the light ivory is on top. Set it down slightly below the dribbles, mash to spread the bristles, and push up into the dribbled paint.

18 Buds are painted with the brush loaded as in step 16. Holding the brush slightly turned so the light ivory side is toward the inside of the bud, begin with pressure at the bottom and pull toward the tip. Use less pressure as you near the end of the stroke. When dry, load the brush as in step 10 and paint the bracts with less pressure for smaller strokes. For the entire ribbon, mix a touch of cobalt blue into light ivory. Load the brush, drag one side through cobalt blue and the other through light ivory. Hold the brush slightly sideways as you paint.

19 The filler flowers are painted with a full load of light ivory. With slight pressure, begin at the outer edge of each petal. Use less pressure as you pull toward the center. This allows the brush to return to a point. After completing all filler flowers, dip the brush handle into yellow oxide and dot in the centers. The stylus is used to make yellow oxide dots in the rose centers. For the decorative stripes, use two rows of masking tape spaced ⅛–¼in (3–5mm) apart and press firmly with the fingers to seal the edges. The space between the tape is painted using the flat brush and dark olive green. Carefully remove the tape as soon as the paint is dry. The corner design is painted with the medium round brush.

20 When the painting is dry, erase all lines and finish with satin or gloss spray or brush-on varnish. For a fine finish use several coats of varnish, allowing each one to dry completely before applying the next. Lightly wet-sand with fine sandpaper, wipe dry, and apply one more coat of varnish.

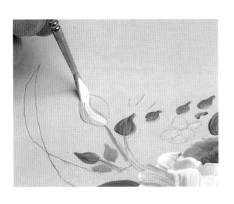

Leather-Look Tilt-Top Table

YOU WILL FIND THIS BEAUTIFUL TABLE IS NOT ONLY A DECORATIVE ACCENT BUT A USEFUL ITEM IN YOUR HOME. HERE FINISHED IN DARK SATIN, ANOTHER COLOR WOULD BE JUST AS LOVELY.

1 Lightly sand and wipe the entire table. With chalk or pencil draw a border 2in (5cm) inside the edge of the table top, using the outer edge as a guide. Stain the border of the table top, the back of the table, and the legs with walnut gel stain. Use a soft, lint-free paper towel or cloth for application, rubbing away the excess with a clean area of the towel or cloth. If a darker color is desired, rub a light amount of black antiquing gel over the stained wood.

2 With the 1in (2.5cm) brush, base coat the table top inside the stained area with gold acrylic paint. When it is dry, a second coat of paint can be applied.

3 Wet the sponge, wring out the excess water and dab one side into the light brown gel stain. Pat on a clean area of the palette to remove any excess. With a slightly rolling motion, pat the gel over the painted section. Allow some of the background to show through. Some areas should be slightly darker than others, so while the light brown gel is still wet, add a bit of walnut brown gel stain to the sponge. Do not overdo; much of the light brown gel and the base coat must be visible.

YOU WILL NEED
Tilt-top table
Sandpaper
Tack cloth
Walnut brown gel stain
Light brown gel stain
Black antiquing gel
Lint-free soft cloth
Gold acrylic paint
Gold metallic paint
Fine-pore synthetic sponge
1in (2.5cm) glazing brush,
large shader (or flat) brush,
small script liner
Satin brush-on or spray varnish
Disposable acrylic paper palette
Paper towels
Chalk or pencil

4 Using the gold metallic paint and the script liner, paint the stroke work around the border. This will clean up any irregularity where the "leather" and stain join. With the shader brush and gold metallic paint, trim along the routed edge of the table top and the edges of the table legs. When all areas are dry, finish with a satin brush-on or spray varnish.

YOU ARE SURE TO WANT SEVERAL OF THESE BEAUTIFUL

CONTAINERS FOR YOUR PATIO OR SUNROOM. MAKE EXTRAS FOR

FRIENDS — ADD A PLANT AND YOU HAVE AN UNUSUAL AND

INEXPENSIVE GIFT THAT WILL BRING YEARS OF PLEASURE.

Angelic
Flower Pot

YOU WILL NEED
Terracotta flower pot
Large shader (or flat) brush,
½in (1cm) stencil brush
Black-green acrylic paint
Gold metallic paint
Crackle medium
Repositionable spray adhesive
Cherub stencil
Stencil brush
Gold foil
Silver foil
Foil adhesive
Exterior varnish

3 Lightly spray the back of the stencil with repositionable spray adhesive. Let it dry for a few moments until it feels sticky but not wet. Blot with a clean, lint-free cloth and position the stencil on the flowerpot. With the stencil brush, pat on a heavy coat of foil adhesive. Carefully remove the stencil so as not to disturb the adhesive and let the glue dry.

1 Base coat the outside of the pot with black-green. Let it dry, then apply a second coat if needed for total coverage. Keep the paint as smooth as possible, avoiding ridges and drips.

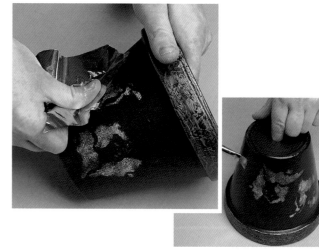

2 Brush a heavy coat of crackle medium over the rim of the pot, using the large flat brush. When it feels tacky to the touch, apply a coat of gold metallic paint over the crackle. Light cracks will be visible when the paint is dry.

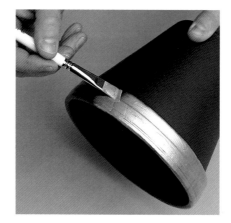

4 Cut the gold foil into smaller pieces and press them firmly over the adhesive. Leave a few small areas unfoiled. Lift the backing paper, leaving foil on areas covered with adhesive. For added interest, press silver foil in the open areas. Finish the pot with a coat of exterior varnish. Let it dry, then apply another coat.

Elegant *Wastebasket*

THIS TECHNIQUE IS GUARANTEED TO PRODUCE DIFFERENT RESULTS EACH TIME YOU USE IT — BUT BE ASSURED THAT YOU WILL BE DELIGHTED WITH ITS STYLISH EFFECT, WHICH IS BOTH QUICK AND EASY TO DO.

YOU WILL NEED
Round wooden wastebasket
Sandpaper
Wood sealer
Tack cloth
Mid-green and viridian acrylic paints
1in (2.5cm) glazing brush
Sea sponge
Crackle medium
Gold water-based spray paint
Gloss spray varnish
Disposable acrylic paper palette
Paste wax

1 Sand and seal the wastebasket. When dry, lightly sand again and wipe away the residue with a tack cloth. Base coat the entire basket using the 1in (2.5cm) brush and mid-green. Remember to paint the inside. Let the paint dry thoroughly.

2 Wet the sponge and wring out the excess water. With the damp sponge, pat viridian over the wastebasket, allowing the base color to show through. When the paint is dry, brush a heavy, even coat of crackle medium over the outside of the wastebasket. Let it dry until it becomes slightly tacky to the touch.

3 Shake the spray paint well and spray randomly over the crackle medium. In some places you will want a heavy coverage, in others less, and in some places very little or none at all.

4 As the crackle medium dries, cracks, starbursts, and other designs will begin to appear. Drying time will vary, but the crackle medium and the paint must be completely dry before going to step 5.

5 Finish with gloss varnish, using several coats inside the wastebasket for protection. A coat of wax on the outside bottom will prevent the wastebasket from sticking to the floor.

123

DECORATIVE FINISHES

Decorative Finishes Gallery

Papier-mâché Vase (right)

This vase was made with a mixture of layered and pulped papier-mâché on a contoured vase as a mold. A layering method was used to create the vase shape, and the pulp was added to embellish it by building up raised areas. The texture of the pulped papier-mâché was enhanced by the paint effect. A base color of blue acrylic paint mixed with a little craft glue was applied. Once dry, a second layer of turquoise acrylic paint was dabbed over random areas using a stencil brush. The texture in the pulp was enhanced by rubbing a small amount red paint over the surface.

Textured Bowl (above)

This decorative bowl was created by molding air-drying clay around a glass cooking bowl. Once dry, the mold was removed and primed using a coat of craft glue painted over the surface. Texture was created in the paint before application by mixing rough-grain sand and craft glue with the turquoise acrylic paint. The mixture was applied thickly with a spatula. Once the surface was covered, random squares were painted around the sides of the bowl using white acrylic paint. While the paint was still wet, lengths of shaped copper wire were pushed in around the squares to create a stitched effect.

Paper Lamp (right)

This unusual, asymmetrical lamp was made using air-drying clay and sculptor's mesh. Three shades of blue tissue paper and beaded-texture gel were used to decorate the base and shade of the uplighter. Tissue paper was torn into strips and applied to the mesh using diluted craft glue. The texture gel was applied to the lamp base and graduated up the sides of the shade. Once dry, random areas of the textured base were highlighted using white and blue acrylic paint brushed lightly over the surface with a dry, flat brush.

Crackled and Decorated Headboard
(*above*)

Some crackle finishes work well as finished effects, some as backgrounds for painted designs, or over decorative treatments such as decoupage. Here, intricate decorative painting has been applied over a striking, blue-green crackle finish.

Spiral Bowl (*left*)

This papier-mâché bowl has been decorated by adding wire spirals and then a paint finish. Once the spirals were attached, the interior was painted using acrylic paint blended with craft glue. Yellow highlights were added to the rim and base, and when dry, red acrylic paint was lightly sponged over the surface.

Index

127

128

Technical terms

This book contains a number of technical terms that may be unfamiliar to readers who have not tried a particular craft technique. Check with your supplier, who should be able to explain or help you find the materials you need.

There may also be words in the book that are unfamiliar to UK readers. The following list gives the UK equivalent for terms that may cause confusion.

US term	UK term
cheesecloth	muslin
cookies	biscuits
cotton swab	cotton bud
flatware	cutlery
pickling gel	liming gel
pressed wood	MDF (fibreboard)
sheet music	music manuscript
steel wool	wire wool
sunroom	conservatory
wastebasket	rubbish bin

Credits

Quarto would like to thank the following project makers for their contributions to the book: Diane Bantz, Ray Bradshaw, Pippa Howes and Peter Knott.

We would like to acknowledge and thank the following artists for allowing us to reproduce their work in this book.

Nadya Derungs (box, page 68, plate, page 69, frames, page 92); Pippa Howes (backgammon board, page 68, vase, bowl and lamp, page 124, bowl, page 125); Peter Knott (oak box, page 53, umbrella stand and marbled bust, page 93); Nancy Snellen (box, page 52, shelf, page 53, plate, page 68, candle box, page 93).

Additional credits: Elizabeth Whiting Associates (verdigris bowls, page 69, decorated headboard, page 125).

All other pictures are the copyright of Quarto Publishing.

Quarto would also like to thank Delta Paints for kindly supplying materials used by the project makers and also in photography.

USA
Delta Technical Coatings
2550 Pellissier Place
Whittier, CA 9060-1505

UK
George Weil & Sons, Ltd
20 Reading Arch Road
Redhill, Surrey RH1 1HJ

We would also like to thank the following suppliers:

Art Craft
415 East 7th Avenue
Joplin, MO 64801, USA

Loew Cornell Brushes
563 Chestnut Avenue
Teaneck, NJ 07666-2490, USA

Jo Sonya Products
Thomas Set & Co
Holly House
Castle Hill
Hartley
Kent DA3 7BH, UK

Scumble Goosie
Suppliers of blanks and materials
Lewiston Mill
Brimscombe
Stroud
Gloustershire, UK